THE WAY
TO
BIBLICAL
PREACHING

THE WAY
TO
BIBLICAL PREACHING

Donald G. Miller

ABINGDON
Nashville

THE WAY TO BIBLICAL PREACHING

Copyright © 1957 by Abingdon Press

All rights in this book are reserved.
No part of the book may be reproduced in any
manner whatsoever without written permission of
the publishers except brief quotations embodied in
critical articles or reviews. For information address
Abingdon, Nashville, Tennessee.

ISBN 0-687-44174-9

Library of Congress Catalog Card Number: 57-11012

Scripture quotations unless otherwise designated are
from the Revised Standard Version of the Bible and
are copyright 1946 and 1952 by the Division of
Christian Education of the National Council of
the Churches of Christ in the U.S.A.

MANUFACTURED BY THE PARTHENON PRESS AT
NASHVILLE, TENNESSEE, UNITED STATES OF AMERICA

DEDICATED

TO

MY WIFE

who
has made a home
whose central meaning has been
Christ
and whose abiding fellowship
has been a foretaste
of the true home of the
soul

PREFACE

Someone has remarked that if Protestantism ever dies with a dagger in its back, the dagger will be the Protestant sermon. If Protestant ministers cannot see more than humor in this, at least those outside the church can. A current literary critic recently wrote concerning a sermon he had heard:

It was based on a pencil. Yes, a pencil. . . . It seems that the graphite, or soul, of a pencil is more important than the wood, or body; and a pencil has an eraser, which has something to do with your sins being blotted out. What pleased me so much was not the sermon itself . . . but the text. In order to give his idea a Scriptural tie-in, the rector took as his text "Pilate answered, What I have written I have written," which gave me a delightful picture of Pilate in his toga chewing the eraser on the end of a modern lead pencil, or even cranking a pencil sharpener.

This work is an effort to help remedy the indictment implied in the foregoing account. It is a sequel to a former book entitled *Fire in Thy Mouth,* in which the philosophy of preaching as redemptive event was the central concern. Much that is assumed in this work is discussed and argued at length in the earlier work, to which reference might well be made as background for what is said here.

I am speaking here, as there, with utmost frankness. Convictions worth holding demand candor in their expression. I cannot ask the reader to agree with me at every point. I can only ask for a thoughtful reading and for the testing of one's disagreement by the biblical revelation.

In order to be as practical as possible and to give point to what is said, I have made reference to many contemporary illustrations of what is actually being done in Protestant pulpits in the name of preaching. I have tried in each case to clothe the examples in anonymity. Some, however, may inadvertently be identified. I can only say that many of these involve my close personal friends, a fact which should indicate that no rancor is involved. And is it a violation of friendship for one to raise the question with another whether, however honest his effort, he has missed the meaning of a passage of scripture? Dwight L. Moody once mumbled while Henry Weston was speaking, "There goes one of my sermons." Weston stopped to inquire what he meant. Moody replied that another of his sermons had just been ruined by an interpretation which had shown his own to be inadequate. This brought no impairment of friendship between the two, but rather deepened it.

In order to maintain anonymity throughout, I have avoided the use of identifying footnotes, although complete documentation could have been given in nearly every case. May I here acknowledge a deep indebtedness to many whose names would otherwise have been mentioned. I cannot avoid, however, mentioning the name of the late James Coffin Stout, formerly a professor at the Biblical Seminary in New York. He it was who first worked out the elements dealt with in Chapters III-VII and set the mind of the present writer going in that direction. I have acknowledged my indebtedness to Dr. Stout in various places in the book, but his contribution to this work transcends these acknowledgments. The use I have made of his material, however, is my own, for which he bears no responsibility.

The major part of this work was first given as the Southwestern Lectures at Southwestern University, Georgetown, Texas, in June, 1955. My special gratitude is due William C. Finch, the president of the university, for the invitation to deliver the lectures and for unnumbered kindnesses to me and my family during our stay in Georgetown. Appreciation is expressed also to those who very graciously listened to the lectures as they were delivered. With additions and some revision these are now sent forth in the hope that they may have some small part in a much-needed recovery of great preaching in Protestantism and may help to answer the ancient prayer of Augustine, quoted in the Preface to the Authorized Version of the Bible: "O let thy Scriptures be my pure delight, let me not be deceived in them, neither let me deceive by them."

DONALD G. MILLER

CONTENTS

INTRODUCTION

Faith Comes by Hearing

———•—•———

Preaching is not mere speech; it is an event. In true preaching, *something happens.* Preacher and people are brought together by the living flame of truth, as oxygen and matter are joined in living encounter by fire. The eternal problem of the preacher is how to produce such a response. Techniques are studied and methods pursued which are designed to work in each succeeding generation. However praiseworthy these may be, preaching can never achieve its true end without a concentration on its message. "Faith comes from what is heard."

But the message does not originate with the preacher. "What is heard comes by the preaching of Christ." Christ was God's event, his historic action in man's behalf. Basically, therefore, Christianity is not a body of ideas, not a way of looking at life, not a philosophy of meaning, not a technique for successful or happy living. It is the story of what God has done for man in Christ. And the story must be told. "Good news" is of something that has happened, and men must know that it has happened.

This means that the message is much more central than either the messenger or the one to whom it is told. True preaching cannot take place until both preacher and listener understand the nature of the gospel with which they are confronted. It is not a mere body of ideas to which men are summoned to assent. It is rather the story of God's personal approach to man in holy action for his salvation, demanding surrender and faith. The central concern of preaching, therefore, is so to rehearse the story of God's redeeming action in Christ that this becomes a living reality in the act of preaching. Therefore, no tricks of the trade, no understanding of psychology, no examination of methods by which men are swayed, can take the place of constant serious study of the historic record of God's redeeming action set forth in the Bible. The preacher must be kept vital as God's redemptive action seizes him anew. The story is not something that a man hears once, then carries in his mind as a memory. It must be heard over and over again, so that in the retelling of it the event comes alive afresh. For the preacher the study of the "gospel" can never be ended.

This means, therefore, that the preacher's study of people and the methods by which he hopes to break into men's lives with the gospel must always be oriented toward the message. Men cannot hear the "good news" that God has done something for them too wonderful to believe, unless they know that they need to have something done for them and have some awareness of what that something is. It is only the gospel which will put them within hearing distance of the gospel! The preacher's task is not so much to show man a way out of his predicament. It is rather to confront him with the radical nature of his predicament.

Man tends to appraise his problem in terms of maladjustment to life, or in terms of personality problems, or economic needs, or health difficulties. He is seeking peace, plenty, health, happiness; and if he cannot find these elsewhere, he may turn to God as their source. The gospel confronts man with a God who is not the source of rest, but first the cause of unrest; not the simple purveyor of peace, plenty, and health, but the One who often invades our lives by smashing all these; not the kindly Father of our dreams who gently caresses our hands, but the

14

God and Father of our Lord Jesus Christ whose only Son had to learn obedience by the things which he suffered, and who often leads us on the same path toward sonship. To communicate the gospel, therefore, is so to confront men with the "good news" that its tragic dimensions make their human tragedies pale into insignificance, and they are led into the awareness that their real need lies in their radical dislocation from God.

The Incarnation, the Cross, and the Resurrection together are parts of the one grand event before which the whole universe is brought to judgment and offered grace. Apart from the limitations of time and space, every life which was ever created would have been literally there gazing on Bethlehem's manger, Golgotha's agony, and the empty tomb in Joseph's garden. Through the retelling of the story, the whole event must be "placarded," re-enacted before the eyes of each successive generation, until they become living participants in both its judgment and its grace. When the ancient Israelites recited in their worship the story of their deliverance by God at the Exodus, it was not the mere recalling of an ancient happening. Each Israelite who heard the story sensed that he was a participant in it, that he as an Israelite lived in the destiny of Israel, that he would not be there recalling the story had not the God who initiated it been at work in Israel's history ever since and were he not active in their behalf even as the story was rehearsed. Likewise, the retelling of the story of God's new deliverance in Jesus on the part of the early church was not a mere rehashing of a past event. It was rather the reconstituting of that event in such a way that it became a current deliverance of those who heard it, making past history for them present event.

Only preaching which sets forth the Bible story can do this. And that which fails to do it is something other than preaching. It is the purpose of this book to try to redefine exposition in terms of content rather than form, showing that all true preaching is the reconstituting in the current moment of the historic deed of redemption witnessed in the Bible, and offering a practical method by which this may be done.

True communication of the gospel is for a preacher so to confront men with "the word of the Cross" that he raises for them poignantly and personally the question of the old Negro spiritual: "Were you there when they crucified my Lord?" and evokes the response: "Yes, I was there!"

I

DEFINING THE TASK

What Is Biblical Preaching?

———•———

Whatever be the marks of the contemporary American pulpit, the centrality of biblical preaching is not one of them. A famine is abroad—"not a famine of bread, nor a thirst for water, but of hearing the words of the Lord" (Amos 8:11).

No doubt there are various reasons for this. One of the chief of them, however, lies in the popular identification of biblical preaching with a rather stereotyped and highly questionable species of expository preaching. If biblical preaching is what most men consider expository preaching to be, they naturally will avoid it. Perhaps the first step in a renewal of true biblical preaching is to break the chains of contemporary association which equate the preaching of the Bible with a false conception of expository preaching. Although the word "expository" in our time may be in disrepute, it is too significant a word to be sacrificed on the altar of misunderstanding. The time has come to restore it to its true significance.

Expository preaching has suffered for years from a widespread misunderstanding of its nature. It has been considered a special type of pulpit discourse, suited only to certain occasions and to be used effectively only by a few ministers who have a rare turn of mind which makes it appealing. In our time it is usually associated with interminable discourses of seventeenth-century Puritans, whose twelve divisions and twenty-seven subdivisions would strain a modern congregation to the breaking point. Or, at best, exposition is considered as a favorite tool of hyperconservative "Bible Conference" leaders, whose method resembles a verse-by-verse running commentary on the various books of the Bible.

This conception has been strangely furthered by countless books on preaching. In the average book on the minister's task in the pulpit, expository preaching is usually dealt with in a few paragraphs or at most a chapter. Even without saying so, this sets it off as an occasional, special type of preaching to which little attention is to be given in the course of a year's pulpit work, and which is comparatively unimportant in the larger area of a minister's concern. Furthermore, some books devoted exclusively to the subject of expository preaching present it as a rather specialized field, a unique skill to be placed alongside other forms of preaching as one among many.

An examination of some definitions of expository preaching suggests how widespread is this narrow conception of it. John A. Broadus wrote: "An expository discourse may be defined as one which is occupied mainly, or at any rate very largely, with the exposition of Scripture." He later sharpens this definition by referring to an expository discourse as one "dealing largely in explanation of the text." This he elaborates by speaking of a "strictly expository sermon" as one "in which not only the leading ideas of the passage are brought out but its details are suitably explained and made to furnish the chief material of the discourse." The weight of Broadus' emphasis seems to set "explanation" over against "application," for he insists that "pains should be taken to point out and apply the lessons which the text may afford." He then adds: "Of course such lessons must, in general, be briefly indicated, as so much time is needed for exposition. But where there is a subject of special practical importance, it may be discussed and urged at length, even if some portions of the text have to be left unexplained." [1]

An analysis of these statements of Broadus shows that from his standpoint the thing which makes a sermon expository is that its major content should be a rather didactic presentation of the meaning of both the leading ideas and the minor details of a passage of Scripture, with some application of these ideas to the contemporary scene made at the proper places.

Another definition is that of Henry Burgess, who says: "Expository preaching consists in taking a certain portion of Scripture, and explaining it without reference to that unity of subject, which we have so much recommended in what is more specially known as a sermon." If this be so, then little is the wonder that many preachers shy away from it! To be expository, one's sermon structure must be primarily explanatory; he must avoid unity and will end up with something other than what may be "specially known as a sermon"!

F. B. Meyer has defined expository preaching as *"the consecutive treatment of some book or extended portion of Scripture* on which the preacher has concentrated . . . until it has yielded up its inner secret, and the spirit of it has passed into his spirit." Here the marks of exposition involve the *length* of the passage handled and a *consecutive* series of sermons on a large segment of scripture. With this conception R. W. Dale would have agreed in his early days (although he later changed his conception), for he spoke of his own expository sermons as those "in which I carefully explained and illustrated, clause by clause, verse by verse, a group of chapters, or a complete book of Holy Scripture."

[1] *On the Preparation and Delivery of Sermons* (rev. ed.; New York: Harper & Bros., 1944), pp. 144, 146, 149.

To give but one current definition of expository preaching, we turn to Andrew W. Blackwood. He writes:

In the broad sense, this sort of sermon is the unfolding of the truth contained in a passage longer than two or three consecutive verses. Often the unit is a single paragraph. Again the chosen passage may be a chapter, or some other cluster of paragraphs. Occasionally the sermon has to do with an entire book of the Bible. . . . According to the present book, therefore, any pulpit message which is based on a fairly long biblical passage is an expository sermon.

A summary of these definitions sets forth the following characteristics of expository preaching. First, there is almost universally an emphasis on the *length* of the passage handled. Broadus dissociates himself from this somewhat by indicating that it may be devoted to a long passage, or to a very short one, albeit his "short" passage might involve at least several verses; but they all seem to be committed to the view that if one should be preaching on but one verse, or a part of a verse, he could not preach a truly expository sermon. Second, *detailed analysis* is stressed, even to the point of verse-by-verse, clause-by-clause treatment. This would seem to suggest that if the details of a passage of scripture were left out of the sermon as it was preached, it would thereby not be expository. The third mark is the *explanatory method of presentation*, as though to be expository is to follow the form of preaching which says in so many words, "This passage means so and so." The fourth element commonly stressed involves the idea of *consecutive handling* of an extended portion of scripture. Accordingly, it would be questionable whether it would be possible to preach just *one* expository sermon to a given congregation at any time. (Broadus, however, admits this possibility.)

It is clear that this narrow conception of exposition is the one popularly held outside the realm of books on preaching.

A recent writer in a reputable periodical, describing London preachers, characterized one whose "special gift is to take a Bible situation and open it up to public view. The 'Bible world' comes alive under him without the perils of biblicism, and at the end of a sermon you know without any shadow of doubt what he has said." This would seem to be a description of a truly expository preacher. But the writer immediately thereafter contrasted him with another clergyman of whom he wrote: "Not far away from this intelligent clarity . . . you will find the expository preaching of ———." Whether he consciously intended it or not, he reflected the currently narrow view of expository preaching as something which is quite limited to a stereotyped manner of presenting consecutive portions of scripture in an explanatory way, which smacks of an uncritical biblicism.

With the limitations thus imposed by these descriptions of expository preaching, it is not surprising that it should be thought of as a form of pulpit discourse suited only to a few ministers whose native gifts enable them to adapt to it or whose outlook is obscurantist. Neither is it surprising that most ministers have "shelved" expository preaching as a relic of by-gone days, which it would be an anachronism to try to restore in the twentieth century. In the light of these definitions of expository preaching, the writer would heartily agree that it has had its day, and that any attempt to restore it to favor would be as pointless as trying to re-establish the use of the old-fashioned spinning wheel or the lamented "surrey with the fringe on top."

The renewal of biblical preaching awaits a clear understanding that to be expository is not to be hampered by such limitations as the above definitions would impose on preaching. Truly biblical exposition is limited only by the broad principle that *the substance of one's preaching should be drawn from the Bible.*

Granted this premise, then it follows that *all true preaching is expository preaching, and that preaching which is not expository is not preaching.*

I have at times hesitated to put the case thus strongly, both because of the possibility of being misunderstood—since we are referring solely to the *substance* and not the *homiletic form* of sermons—and because of the seeming novelty of the view—novel, that is, to our time, although I am convinced that it is but the recovery of the original Reformation conception of preaching. I have been encouraged, however, to state the issue thus squarely by finding it boldly argued in print by another writer who could not be accused of committing himself to unwholesome novelties. Marvin R. Vincent, known to the present generation of ministers largely through his much-used volumes entitled *Word Studies in the New Testament,* wrote another work called *The Expositor in the Pulpit,* which seems to have fallen out of circulation. In this work he wrote that "the phrase 'Expository Preaching' properly covers *all* preaching. Exposition is *exposing* the truth contained in God's word: *laying it open; putting it forth* where the people may get hold of it; and that also is preaching."

The truth or falsity of this view depends on one's conception of what preaching is. If a sermon is what one writer has defined as "a disquisition on some moral or spiritual truth in which the preacher sets forth his own heartfelt convictions and by which he hopes to interest the intellect, awaken the conscience, and touch the hearts of his hearers," then it may be a man-centered affair from start to finish with no relationship whatsoever to the Word of God set forth in Holy Scripture. Thus one could preach without drawing the substance of his preaching from the Bible. But so could a Buddhist, a Mohammedan, a Hindu, or a pantheist. They, and countless others, have a body of "moral or spiritual truth" which they hold with "heartfelt conviction" and by which they hope "to interest the intellect, awaken the conscience, and touch the hearts" of all who will listen. Much so-called Christian preaching is just this—and nothing more. But has not the time come to ask ourselves whether this can rightly be called preaching in the Christian sense of the term?

One of America's leading preachers, who influences the preaching of a great many others, published a sermon not long ago which illustrates the point at issue. He had taken a trip to Japan, where he saw over and over again the artistic motif of three trees—the pine, the bamboo, and the plum. The answer to his inquiry for an explanation of this motif gave him the substance of a sermon. The structure of the sermon was as follows:

> I. STRENGTH—The pine, because it lives a long time, represents strength.
>
> II. RESILIENCY—The bamboo represents resiliency, for when it is bent low by the storm it does not break, but straightens up again.
>
> III. COURAGE—The plum represents courage, for it is the first to put forth its blooms in the spring and is sometimes brave enough to show its flowers before the snow has quite gone.

There was no text from the Bible, save a casual remark that this Japanese motif made the preacher think of the words of the psalmist, "And he shall be like a tree planted by the rivers of water," nor was there any development of the points within a biblical framework of thought. Strength, resiliency, and courage may be inculcated as moral virtues by a devotee of a pagan religion or the henchmen of a totalitarian dictator. They are not in themselves distinctively Christian qualities. It is, therefore, not surprising that two of the chief illustrations of these virtues were the way the Japanese took their defeat in

World War II and the success with which Disraeli surmounted his handicaps—both of whom had the virtue extolled without benefit of the Christian faith. "We do not grow Christians," said Edward Irving, "by the same culture by which we grow men, otherwise what need of divine revelation, and divine assistance?" Strength, resiliency, and courage, from the standpoint of the Christian faith, are not virtues to be cultivated by mere human effort, but the outgrowth in character of the soul's response of faith in a unique gospel—the redeeming act of God in Jesus Christ—who works his work of grace in our souls.

The question arises, therefore, whether this type of preaching can lay claim to being Christian preaching at all. If it can, then the thesis here set forth is of little consequence. If, on the other hand, one begins with the conviction that true preaching involves an unfolding of the Word of God in Holy Scripture, made effectual in the hearts of the hearers by the Holy Spirit—so that it is not merely the "heartfelt conviction" of the preacher who hopes to influence human action in one form or another, but becomes the Word of God himself confronting the hearer with both judgment and redemption—then the view here taken is not so novel as it may at first sound. To preach is to bear witness to the unique action of God in Jesus Christ as it is set forth in the record of that action—the Bible—so that the judgment and redemption enacted in those historic deeds become current realities to the soul. If this be granted, it is another way of saying that all true preaching is expository in the broad meaning here intended, in that it is in substance a setting forth of truths drawn from the Bible in a form intelligible and relevant to the needs of men today.

We are now in a position to try to set forth more positively some definition of expository preaching which will state it in its broadest terms. One of the clearest approaches to this was made by Alfred E. Garvie, when he wrote:

[The Christian preacher] will aim at being an expository preacher, not in the narrow sense of always expounding in detail a passage of Scripture, but in the broad sense that even when he deals with a subject, that subject will be connected by no forced exegesis, but by natural affinity with his text, and that the context historically studied will determine his treatment of his text.

Here the length of the passage is irrelevant, detailed analysis is decried, there is no hint that expository preaching must be limited to the explanatory method of presentation, nor is there any suggestion that there must be the consecutive handling of a lengthy section of the Bible. What is insisted upon, however, is that the thought of the sermon should come naturally out of a passage of scripture and that it should be controlled at every point by adequate historical study of the larger setting of which it is a part, so that the true meaning of the passage shall guide the thought of the preacher in every detail of his development.

Another succinct definition of expository preaching was given by James Coffin Stout as follows: "An exposition of any portion of Holy Scripture is such a setting forth of the truth or truths contained therein as shall *justly* reflect its teachings." Here again the length of the passage involved is irrelevant—"any portion"—and there is no suggestion of method or form of presentation, nor any insistence on the limiting marks that the earlier definitions of exposition stressed. Emphasis is placed on the fact that the substance of an expository sermon should be a true reflection of the biblical passage on which it is based, and the way whereby this is to be achieved is the same route as that suggested by Garvie—"the context historically studied." For Stout continues: "Note the stress on the word 'justly.' The whole definition really hinges on this word. . . . 'Justly' involves [the passage's] inter-relations with the surrounding thoughts, its dependence on them, its outgrowth from them." Should any-one miss in this definition the note of application, it also is inherent in the word "justly," for truth in the Bible is never a mere object of contemplation, but is rather the approach of the living God demanding decision. To be confronted by the truth in the biblical sense is to be confronted by God in Christ demanding repentance and faith and commitment. Justly to reflect the truth of the Scriptures, then, means the application of truth to vital relations from start to finish.

We are ready now to attempt a definition of our own, growing out of these others and seeking to make explicit certain aspects which are merely implicit in them. *Expository preaching is an act wherein the living truth of some portion of Holy Scripture, understood in the light of solid exegetical and historical study and made a living reality to the preacher by the Holy Spirit, comes alive to the hearer as he is confronted by God in Christ through the Holy Spirit in judgment and redemption.*

The following elements are here involved: Preaching is not mere speaking; it is an *act*. It accomplishes something. It never leaves a man where it finds him, but makes him either better or worse. Preaching should be founded on the Bible, which is the unique record of God's unique redemptive deed in Christ and which becomes the source and norm for all Christian preaching. The *substance* of preaching, drawn from the Scriptures, is to be found by painstaking study in the light of the best available methods of historical and exegetical research, but this process must be quickened by the living Spirit of God who desires to speak now through his ancient witnesses. The *end* of preaching is that the sermon situation should be transformed from a human encounter between the preacher and his congregation into a divine encounter between God and both preacher and people. Since that which makes preaching what it is, is less its form than its substance, this allows for almost infinite variety of homiletic form in true expository preaching. A sermon may be life-situational, doctrinal, evangelistic, or ethical, and still be

26

expository if its approach to the subject is rooted in the Scriptures, and it throws true biblical light on the contemporary scene.

If this broad definition of expository preaching be accepted, then it remains true that *all* real preaching is expository preaching; for if a pulpit discourse does not embody the elements included in our definition, it can hardly be classed as a sermon, but becomes rather a lecture or an address. The ancient categories, therefore, of topical, textual, and expository are irrelevant from the standpoint of determining the biblical content of a sermon. Whatever validity they may have in the jargon of formal homiletic technique, they can do little but create mischief when they are used to delineate the relative biblical content of a sermon. Insofar as a topical sermon is considered one which does not necessarily draw its substance from the Bible, and a textual sermon is considered one which is based on the wording of a specific text taken out of its setting in the Bible, and an expository sermon is thought of as one whose form is determined by a relatively long passage of scripture but does not really convey what that passage originally meant, great harm has been the result.

It is this which has given many ministers the feeling that the exposition of the Scriptures is not their primary and continual task in the pulpit. Consequently, they frequently select topics which they do not relate in any vital way to the Scriptures and on which they offer the listeners nothing but their own best thought, and feel that they have preached a topical *sermon*. Or they may take a text quite unrelated to anything they have to say, save that its wording suggests some picture or framework into which they may pour their own ideas, and feel that they have preached a textual *sermon*. Sometimes, too, men preach what they call an expository sermon, in which they roam back and forth through a long passage of scripture, quote and requote, and utilize the larger sweep of a passage to illustrate or justify a structure of theology which they brought with them to the passage, but which bears no vital relationship to what the passage actually meant to the original writer—and conclude that they have thereby preached an expository *sermon*. This sort of preaching, although expository in name, may be as far from true biblical preaching as the brashest sort of topical or textual manipulation. True exposition of the Scriptures must be rescued from all three of these aberrations. It must be based on a serious wrestling with the Word of God in the Scriptures, until its substance is controlled at every point by the record of the unique redemptive acts of God in the history of Israel and of the early church.

From the standpoint of the witness of both the early church and the Reformation church, many modern pulpit efforts, although often brilliant and humanly satisfying, would have been considered an impertinence—the intrusion of the word of a mere man into a situation where God alone has the right to speak. In the words of the writer of Second Timothy, this would have been considered the exchange of "the word of truth" for "godless chatter" which does not make "the man of God . . . complete" or equip him "for every good work." Insofar as this has arisen through the popular distinction between topical, textual, and expository preaching, it is essential that these categories be abandoned. Our salvation at this point lies in a new understanding of what exposition is, and a new confrontation with the fact that unless preaching involves a serious wrestling with biblical truth, it is not preaching at all. This may seem radical, but radical diseases often demand radical cures.

A topical discussion which is not at the same time an exposition of scripture is not really a topical sermon. If the topic of a sermon is the topic of the passage on which it is based, and if this topic is developed in such a way that it sets forth the true meaning of the passage, understood in its context in the light of historical and exegetical study, then and only then is it a topical sermon. But a sermon that is topical in this sense is also an exposition of scripture. To be topical, therefore, without being at the same time expository, is to make a religious address rather than a sermon.

A good example of this sort of so-called topical preaching may be seen in a sermon based on an abbreviated form of Heb. 2:1: "Pay the closer attention . . . lest we drift away." The only connection discernible between the text and the sermon was in the title, "The Ebb Tide." The word "drift" in the text suggested this title. The structure of the sermon was as follows:

> Introduction: Many powerful currents are moving through modern life which are sucking us away from our moorings. Drifting with these currents, we are headed for possible destruction.
>
> I. We are drifting away from *love*. Since Christian love is the essence of democracy, we are likely to lose our political heritage in hatred of others.
>
> II. We are drifting away from *faith in the future*. Our cynicism in many realms testifies to this.
>
> III. We are drifting away from *faith in God*. This is evidenced by the fact that Brooklyn, once the city of churches in the days of Beecher, Talmage, Cuyler, and Storrs, now has an average attendance in each church of little more than 160. If a decline such as this continues, Protestantism may die out.

Here are three observations on modern life made by the preacher. They might conceivably be the result of his looking out on life through Christian eyes and from the perspective of a biblical faith. But there is no explicit connection made between the sermon and the biblical passage on which it was allegedly preached, and certainly no distinctively Christian appeal such as the author of Hebrews was making. The writer of Hebrews was warning his readers of the danger of drifting away from a "great salvation" which they had heard from the lips of those who had received it from Jesus and which had been confirmed to them by the working of the Holy Spirit. It was not love as the essence of democracy nor faith in the future from which they were drifting, but the gospel of God in Jesus Christ. And the fearfulness of their drift lay not in the fact that democracy might fall on hard days or that the future of the social order might suffer, but in the fact that they were neglecting a salvation wrought for them by One who was now seated on the right hand of God, to whom all things had been subjected and to whom alone their loyalty belonged. The topical approach, which had nothing to do with the text, was merely the logical arrangement of certain ideas in the preacher's mind gathered around a figure of speech suggested by the biblical passage. But it must be asked whether a Christian pulpit is the appropriate place for such an exercise. And dare we call it a sermon?

This same question must be raised with regard to many so-called textual sermons. Is a textual discussion which is unrelated to the meaning of the text used really a textual sermon? The answer would seem to be obvious. To compose a sermon which consists of thoughts suggested to the mind of the preacher by the wording of a text, but which have no true relation to what the text means may, from the point of view of formal homiletic structure, be called textual, but in reality it is no textual sermon at all. An illustration will make this clear.

Some years ago there appeared a multivolumed work entitled *The World's Great Sermons*. In one of the volumes there is a sermon entitled "The Prepared Worm," based on Jonah 4:7: "But God prepared a worm when the morning rose the next day, and it smote the gourd that it withered." (K.J.V.) The theme of the sermon is suggested by a sentence near the close of the introduction: "Let us endeavour to understand some of the facts connected with our afflictions, as disclosed by the Word of God." Biblical light on human affliction is the purported theme drawn from this passage. The points are as follows.

I. "God is the author of affliction"—"*God* prepared a worm." God "could prevent affliction, but he permits it." Satan is the real source of injuries, but God allows them "in order to remove our affections from the world" and set them on him.

II. God "uses the natural laws of the world as his agents in afflicting"—"God prepared a *worm*." This point is elaborated by observations on nature, showing how in both her beautiful as well as her ugly moods, nature is the scene of God's working.

III. "God is just in afflicting us." In the discussion of this point no significant reference is made to the passage.

IV. "God afflicts us in his love." The worm was prepared not to punish Jonah, but to cast him back on God. "If we can learn our lesson without the worm, the worm will not be sent to gnaw our gourd to ruins."

V. Conclusion—some inferences drawn from the above.

A. "If God afflicts," it is foolish "to go to the world for relief."

B. "If God prepares worms, then worms at once form an interesting study for us." We ought to learn all we can about nature.

C. "When our gourds wither, it is proof that God is near."

This is certainly a textual discussion which is not expository. It is highly doubtful that it could justly be called a textual sermon. In the book of Jonah, the preparation of a worm to destroy the gourd is a necessary detail in the story, bearing no theological weight whatsoever. The writer of the book of Jonah would have been startled to have learned that anyone could have read theological implications of this sort into this part of his story. Furthermore, the book of Jonah in the large, and this specific passage in particular, have nothing whatsoever to do with the question of human afflictions.

The book is a dramatic challenge to a narrow theology which had developed in Israel. On the basis of this theology, many had the complacent feeling that God loved Israel but did not love non-Israelites. The tragic consequence of this was that Israel had lost her sense of mission to the world and was failing to enter into the purpose of the Covenant made with her, that in her "all nations" should be blessed. Israel was trying to get God to serve her in political deliverance, instead of being God's servant to bring spiritual deliverance to the rest of the world. The growth and sudden decay of the gourd is a dramatic device to give point to the main drive of the book. If Jonah were piteous of the gourd, which he had not created, for which he had not labored, and which had at best a transient existence, ought not God to be concerned for the Ninevites, pagan though they were, whom he had created, for whose salvation he had labored, and whose destiny was an eternal one?

The gourd, then, in the Jonah passage has nothing to say about afflictions. It is merely a dramatic setting to state what was a breath-taking challenge to the orthodox theology of many of the Israelites of that day: that God was the God of the Ninevites as well as of the Israelites; that God was not the enemy of their enemies, but loved them with the same supreme concern with which he loved Israel. A true textual sermon on this text would of necessity have developed the thought along this general line and would therefore have been biblical, in that it would have set forth the true meaning of the text and drawn from it the substance of the thought of the one who wrote it. As the sermon lies, it is in homiletic form textual, but in substance it is not textual and therefore not exposition of the Scriptures.

It is possible, even, for a sermon that is expository in form to be quite wide of true exposition of scripture. Such preaching thereby falls under the suspicion that it is not preaching at all in the sense laid down earlier in the chapter, but is merely using the Scriptures as a scaffolding from which to erect the human fancies of the preacher. These human fancies may even be suggested by the wording of the scripture on which the so-called expository sermon is allegedly based. But even though a sermon should follow quite closely the biblical wording, yet miss the biblical meaning, it is not truly an expository sermon. One example will be sufficient to illustrate how easily this may take place.

Some years ago a sermon was preached on Ps. 19, which purported to be an expository sermon. The theme was stated in the form of a question: "Why Do We Believe in God?" Its development was somewhat as follows:

Why Do We Believe in God?

I. We believe in the existence of God because of the *number of the reporters.*

    A. The world of nature declares the existence of God (vss. 1-6).

    B. The world of man declares the existence of God (vs. 14).

II. We believe in the existence of God because of the *quality of the reporters.*

    A. "The law of the Lord is perfect" (vs. 7*a*). This is God's revelation in the Old and New Testaments.

    B. "The testimony of the Lord is sure, making wise the simple" (vs. 7*b*). This is God's witness in "his people."

    C. "The precepts of the Lord are right" (vs. 8*a*). This is the testimony of a "righteous man."

    D. "The commandment of the Lord is pure" (vs. 8*b*). This is the testimony of the "saved."

    E. "The fear of the Lord is clean, enduring for ever" (vs. 9*a*). (No identification of the witness was made here.)

    F. "The ordinances of the Lord are true, and righteous altogether" (vs. 9*b*). The testimony of "ourselves as Christians."

III. We believe in the existence of God because of the *difference a belief in God makes in the believer.*

A. Causes believer to see himself as a sinner (vs. 12). "Who can discern his errors?"

B. Causes believer to want to be upright (vs. 13). "Keep back thy servant also from presumptuous sins."

C. Causes believer to want to be acceptable in God's sight (v. 14). "Let the words of my mouth and the meditation of my heart be acceptable in thy sight."

Here are all the formal marks of exposition, according to current ideas of it. The sermon is based on a lengthy passage. It includes not only the larger aspects of the psalm, but the smaller details. It is explanatory in method, trying to set forth what each verse of the psalm means in Christian experience. But is its substance really drawn from Ps. 19? In the first place, the theme is quite other than that of the psalm. Neither here nor elsewhere in the Bible do the writers ever argue for the existence of God. They assume it. In the second place, the points made under the theme are quite other than the substance of the psalm. Under point II, for example, all the aspects of verses 7-10 of the psalm were applied to people, whereas in the psalm these have to do with God's law rather than with persons. In the third place, the personal excellencies described in the closing verses of the psalm are not set forth as evidences for belief in God, but are rather the inner yearning of a devout man that his life should reflect something of the character of the God whom he worshiped. Here, then, is a sermon expository in form but not in substance, suggesting how easy it is to seem to be biblical in one's preaching, yet to miss the drive of biblical truth.

Although illustrations could be multiplied indefinitely, enough has been said to establish the point that so-called preaching which is merely topical, textual, or expository in form, but is unrelated to the thought of the scripture passages on which it is allegedly based, can hardly be called preaching in the true sense of the word. All true preaching, whatever its homiletic form, ought to do what *Webster's New International Dictionary* gives as the meaning of the word "expound"—"to lay open the meaning of" the Word of God in the Bible.

II

STUDYING A PASSAGE

Approach

It may be well, before dealing with the various specific elements which go into the making of a biblical exposition, to face very practically the question of how one goes about studying in preparation for a Bible-centered ministry.

First of all, it is fitting to suggest that for most ministers, at least, the beginnings of their study will be through the medium of their mother tongue. This is based on the principle that the natural avenue of both impression and expression is the language to which one is born. It is the very exceptional thing for a student to acquire a sufficient mastery of another language to be able to think in the patterns of that language. Words and expressions in another tongue ofttimes have a flavor which can be grasped only by those who have spoken the language from childhood or who have for years lived in a milieu where it was spoken constantly.

Many are the stories of those who have acquired a fair speaking knowledge of a foreign tongue, who yet miss its delicate nuances. A Japanese student, for instance, wishing to be exceptionally polite to an English-speaking teacher, addressed him: "August and awful sir!" An Indian language-teacher, wishing to congratulate an American lady who had shown exceptional ability under his tutelage to master the Urdu language, sent her a bouquet of flowers to which he had attached the note: "These, dear lady, will fade and die, but you will smell forever!" Such blunders, of course, are a two-way proposition, and many a citizen of foreign lands has had a good laugh at Americans who have been notorious for their failure to master other tongues.

But even when a large measure of facility has been acquired in a foreign tongue, still the mother tongue is a more effective channel of communication. An American teacher who had grown up in India once told me that in teaching Indian college girls, who had spoken English from the grade-school level and who had certainly a better mastery of English than we could ever get of Greek or Hebrew, it was difficult to teach the Bible in English. In spite of their excellent knowledge of English, they tended to literalize poetic figures of speech and had great difficulty in understanding the flavor of certain idiomatic expressions which suggest more than they say. Since the teacher herself had spoken Urdu as a child before she had spoken English, she used it as her mother tongue. She finally resorted, therefore, to teaching the Bible in Urdu instead of English.

This means that for English-speaking ministers, the most effective place to begin the study of the Bible is in the English versions. In this way, the scripture can make its most effective initial impact, and the student may see it in large relations, with the mind free to grapple with the ideas expressed rather than straining itself with the problems of translation. But as soon as one takes up the serious study of a passage in the English, he will discover problems arising which the English itself cannot answer. What is the exact meaning of certain words? What tense forms lie behind the English translation? What ancient customs or patterns of thought are alluded to? Such questions as these immediately drive one back to the original languages for answer. So, although the English versions form the starting point, one's study does not stop there. Sir Edwyn Hoskyns, one of England's greatest New Testament scholars, used to insist that "the Gospels are strange to us men of the twentieth century, and that to pass the gulf which separates us from them is an infinitely difficult task. Learning Greek is part of that task. The strange language is a symbol of the strangeness of thought that must be passed through before we can understand the Gospels aright." Hence, even though Dean Inge's statement may be true—that "no book loses by translation so little as the New Testament"—yet those whose major task it is to interpret the deeper things of scripture should, if at all possible, seek to have some competence in discovering meanings which the English cannot quite convey.

To make some use of the original languages one does not need to be an expert in them. One of the tragedies of theological education is that many, upon completing their training, feel that since they are not expert linguists, they can make no use of the original languages, and forever lay them aside as tools of study. This might be avoided if it were clearly seen that one may make good use of the languages without being a gifted linguist. As long as one can use a lexicon and a concordance for determining the meaning of words; handle the tools which will enable him to identify a form, the force of which may be checked in a good reference grammar; and understand the evidence set forth in commentaries based on the original languages, he can be something of an independent student and can immeasurably enrich his study of the Bible by even a cumbersome resort to these tools.

Armed with the mother tongue and whatever facility in the biblical languages he may possess, the minister should first of all try to set the study of any particular passage of scripture in its large relations. There is what might be called a "biblical context" which is relevant to understanding any specific area of scripture. The more, therefore, one keeps alive his reading of the entire Bible, the better able he is to grasp the intent of any individual passage.

In addition to the total biblical context in which the thought of the biblical writers moves, it is well always to try to get some grasp of the whole book of which any particular passage is a part. In the main, the books of the Bible are individual units in themselves, each having an individuality of its own. To be fair to any one of these books, it is necessary to try to relate the parts of it to the whole. For what a writer is trying to do in any specific passage may be determined largely by the place that passage holds in the larger unity of the book.

An architect must always keep each item related to the plan for the whole building. Floor plans must be geared in with roof plans. The features of individual rooms must be related to the other rooms of the building. What one desires to do interiorly must be controlled by its relation to the exterior of the building. Writers, too, are architects. Great literary works usually have a unity from which each part takes its meaning. It is well, therefore, to begin the study of a book of the Bible by a search for its ground plan, by a recognition of its larger structural features. Can the purpose of the author be discovered? Is it possible to find any clues to the plan by which he hoped to achieve this purpose? Can it be determined from what viewpoint the writer was looking at his subject matter, so that the reader may look at it from the same point of view? Such questions as these should be asked about a particular book of the Bible before the significance of any single episode in it may fairly be appraised.

Such procedure is patent in the study of art. Composition involves putting things together in such a fashion that each part takes its meaning from every other part and from the purpose of the whole. Take, for example, Johann Hofmann's painting of Christ and the Rich Young Man. There are but four characters in the picture, two of them grouped into a unity of their own. At the right of the picture is the handsomely dressed rich young man. Standing with hand on hips, he is looking disdainfully down at something. If you take this figure out of its relation to the rest of the picture, what does it mean? Well, try it, and you will see that it can mean almost anything—or nothing. Perhaps the young man is reproving a servant who has displeased him. Or perhaps he is disdainfully rejecting the price set upon an oriental rug by a merchant. By itself, it conveys no sure meaning. Turn then to the left corner of the picture. There is a helpless old crippled beggar, hovered over by a young girl who may be his daughter. Take these two out of the picture by themselves, and what do they mean? Artistically, they can mean little or nothing in isolation. Then take the central figure, Jesus, and lift it out of the painting. This is often done, for frequently the head of Christ from this painting is displayed alone. What does it mean? It is just a rather strong face of a man looking at something. Who is the man? At what is he looking? What causes the particular expression on his face? One can answer none of these questions when the face of Jesus is detached from its setting in the unity of the whole picture.

Now, put these isolated units together. In the lower left-hand corner, represented by the cripple and his daughter, there is an ugly picture of human need—the pathos of helpless mankind, diseased and broken, with no balm for its wounds. To the right of the picture is the richly dressed young man. Here are abundant resources which, if touched into life by Christ and used selflessly in the service of others, may be used by God both for the redemption of the needy and the salvation of the one who gives. What is the link between the need and the resources? It is Jesus. With challenge and entreaty His gaze is penetrating to the deeps of the rich young man's soul, while His hands point tenderly toward the needy couple hovering below. It is a simple, yet profound, painting, with each figure taking its artistic meaning from its relationship to the whole.

Books, likewise, often have a unity which must be recognized if the individual parts are not to be robbed of their meaning. It is the initial task of the interpreter, therefore, to search for the purpose and plan of the whole book before coming to grips with its parts. Failure to do this is often fatal to true interpretation. Take, for example, the prayer of intercession made by Abraham in Gen. 18. One frequently hears this incident dealt with entirely apart from the unity of the book of Genesis, in which it is recorded, with the result that a meaning is deduced which was likely quite foreign to the thought of the writer. We are told that Abraham stopped praying too soon. His faith was not strong enough. If he had only lowered his figures further and held on longer, his prayer might have saved Sodom. Hence, the incident is used to point out a religious weakness in the life of a great Old Testament worthy and to counsel the hearer against a like weakness in his own prayer life.

Was this the intention of the editor of Genesis? A look at the whole book indicates that this episode is a part of a great contrast between Abraham and his nephew Lot, who serves throughout the story as a foil for Abraham. At the command of God, Abraham has embarked on a great spiritual venture, through which he was given to believe that somehow "all nations" would be blessed. He is to father a movement which shall ultimately have redemptive significance for all mankind. Lot, on the other hand, shows no signs of having been gripped by this spiritual ideal and is quite content with his "flocks, and herds, and tents." The news comes to Abraham that Sodom is to be destroyed. Why should he care? He does not live there.

42

He is not related to them by blood. He has no business associates among the Sodomites. He knows that they have been wicked and likely deserve the divine judgment. The only point of contact he has with Sodom is through his unworthy nephew, Lot, for whom he has risked his neck once before because of his involvement with Sodom. What is it to Abraham that Sodom is to be destroyed? The whole town may burn up without his losing a single thing. And yet, with almost unparalleled selflessness, Abraham wrestles with God in prayer to try to save unworthy Sodom. Here you have the father of the "nation" which is to bless "all nations" already assuming a spiritually responsible role in human society. His destiny is not for himself, but for the wicked who do not know God as he does.

But what of Lot? Thus far in the story, he has shown himself to be a genial materialist, not outwardly vicious, but living quite solely for himself. He has not sensed the spiritual meaning of his existence. He has lived in a fatal compromise with evil. He has evaluated every experience as an opportunity for self-advancement. Now, in this crisis, he is put to the test, and the real quality of his soul becomes manifest. The word comes to him, too, that Sodom is to be destroyed. Should he be concerned? Yes, quite so. He has lived for a good many years in Sodom. Those to be destroyed are his neighbors. His daughters have been betrothed to Sodomite youths. He has done business with the Sodomites and prospered because of their society. Should he be concerned when the news comes to him that Sodom is to be destroyed? Yes, exceedingly so. But is he?

The only prayer recorded in the book of Genesis from the lips of Lot is the expression of consummate selfishness. When the messengers of God urge him to flee to the hills for safety, he replies: "Oh, no, my lords; . . . I cannot flee to the hills. . . . Behold, yonder city is near enough to flee to, and it is a little one. Let me escape there—is it not a little one?—and my life will be saved!" The whole city can go up in smoke as far as he is concerned, just so he saves his own skin! And he does not want to be too inconvenienced in the doing of it. Since he is a city boy, he insists that he must be saved in a city rather than be subjected to the hardships of the hills! He will selfishly choose even the terms on which life is offered him.

In the light of all this, was the story of Abraham's prayer inserted in the book of Genesis in order for us to moralize on the weakness of his faith or on the lack of persistence in his intercession? Hardly. The story was inserted in order to contrast Lot's utter selfishness with the concern of Abraham for the salvation of others for whom, humanly speaking, he had no responsibility whatsoever. And this was written not just to point out a feature in the character of Abraham, but to remind Israel that her destiny was to live for "all nations" and that she could fulfill her calling only as she abandoned her efforts at self-survival and a place in the sun to become the servant of God for the redemption of the world. It takes some knowledge of the larger structure of the book of Genesis to give meaning to this one episode.

It is well, therefore, to keep one's reading of the whole Bible going quite beyond the specific preparation for weekly sermons. In this way the larger relations of the various books of the Bible become increasingly familiar, and whenever one dips into any specific passage, he can immediately set it in its relation to the rest of the book of which it is a part. General Bible study contributes increasingly to sermon preparation.

After an effort has been made to grasp the unifying features of the whole book, the next step is to come to grips with the specific area of scripture on which one plans to prepare a sermon. A beginning may be made here by setting the limits of the context. We have already mentioned the total biblical context and the context of the entire book. The third context involves the immediate materials which surround the specific words which form the text. One must ask himself: "How far back and how far forward must I go to be sure that I have grasped the real significance of these words?" Sometimes one does not need to go very far. Just the completion of a verse would have saved the preacher from developing the theme. "The Preciousness of the Word of God," from I Sam. 3:1: "And the word of the Lord was precious in those days." The rest of the verse reads: "There was no open [frequent] vision." (K.J.V.) This defines immediately the connotation of the word "precious"—it means "precious scarce," or rare. And Samuel was called to be a channel through which the word of the Lord might come again to his people in freshness and power.

Sometimes the immediate paragraph in which the text comes is sufficient, as in the passage, Phil. 3:8: "Indeed I count everything as loss because of the surpassing worth of knowing Christ Jesus my Lord. For his sake I have suffered the loss of all things, and count them as refuse, in order that I may gain Christ." Here the paragraph opens with a reference to "the dogs," the members of the circumcision party, "who mutilate the flesh." It ends with a reference to Paul's desire to have no righteousness of his own "based on law, but that which is through faith in Christ." The thought of the entire paragraph is sufficient to define what the "all things" were that Paul counted as "loss." At still other times it may be necessary to peruse a whole chapter or a larger segment of a book in order to be sure that one is moving in line with the thought of the author at any given point.

The next step is to work with the major words used in the passage—both text and context. Words are symbols of meaning in the mind of the author and can rightly be interpreted not by putting into them what they mean to us, but by investigating what they meant to the one who used them. It is at this point that some use of the original languages, for those who have any tools for them at all, is indispensable. And almost anyone can take the trouble, whether he knows the languages himself or not, to check in one or two standard commentaries, in order to define the terms as best he can with the aid of the commentators. Failure to do this may often cause us to misrepresent the thought of the biblical writers. The importance of this we should perhaps not stress in quite the same fashion as did Nathaniel J. Burton in his Yale Lectures of 1872, but his word may well be heeded:

Now you see in a moment that in order to the truthful use of language, we are carried directly to philological and exegetical study. All people would agree that preachers need to be up in those studies as a matter of information; but I say unto you to-day it is a matter of integrity also. What is slander? Well, one form of it is reporting that a man said something that he did not say. And why is not the Bible slandered when some inaccurate and unexegetical fumbler spends hours every week in public discoursings on what the Bible says? . . .

So then our very veracity forces us to philology, to exegesis, to profound interpretation. If we intentionally misrepresent meanings, we are liars, plain as day. But if we misrepresent meanings through carelessness, or through laziness, it shows that we have in us the making of a liar. We are willing to make statement after statement that we have never taken the trouble to verify.

At least four channels are open to investigate word meanings. The first is the use of lexicons, where exact definitions are to be found. Henry Liddell and Robert Scott's *Greek-English Lexicon* serves well in indicating root meanings. Joseph H. Thayer's *Greek-English Lexicon of the New Testament* and Friedrich H. W. Gesenius' *Hebrew and Chaldee Lexicon to the Old Testament Scriptures* are old classics for the study of biblical words. Two recent works are fuller and more up-to-date:

Ludwig Koehler's *Lexicon in Veteris Testimenti Libros: A Dictionary of the Hebrew Old Testament in English and German,* and a translation of Walter Bauer's lexicon by W. F. Arndt and F. W. Gingrich, under the title, *A Greek-English Lexicon of the New Testament and Other Early Christian Literature.*

But definition alone is not sufficient to determine the meaning of words. Usage is even more important. Words have not only denotation; they have also connotation. What they mean on the lips of people or in the pages of literature is often more determinative of their significance than what the lexicon has to say. Contrast, for example, the poet's description of a kiss with that of a dictionary. To determine the meaning of a word through usage, a concordance is indispensable. In some ways a good concordance is perhaps one of the most fruitful tools available for the study of the Bible. Bishop Westcott once wrote: "Patient students of the New Testament will, I think, agree that they have not found any commentary so fruitful as a concordance." One could almost construct his own dictionary through the use of a concordance, and a fruitful mind could utilize it in preparing his own commentary. Salomon Mandelkern's *Concordance to the Old Testament* and either William Moulton and Alfred Geden's *Concordance to the Greek Testament* or *The Englishman's Greek Concordance* published by Bagster will prove helpful. If these are not available, or if the student has no knowledge of the original languages, much may be accomplished through the use of James Strong's *Exhaustive Concordance of the Bible,* or Robert Young's *Analytical Concordance to the Bible,* both of which have aids in determining the original words behind the English. J. B. Smith's *Greek-English Concordance to the New Testament* is a remarkably worked-out aid for English readers; it indicates the Greek words behind the English expressions and charts the frequency and

47

location of all the words in graphic form—which saves hours of search on the part of the student.

When several significant usages have been checked with the aid of a concordance to sharpen the understanding of a particular word, the third source of information on words is word-study books. Of these the most thorough is Gerhard Kittel's *Theologisches Wörterbuch zum Neuen Testament,* several articles of which have been translated into English under the general title *Bible Key Words.* The translation of other articles is promised for the future. Other helpful works are Richard C. Trench, *Synonyms of the New Testament;* Alan Richardson, *A Theological Word Book of the Bible;* William Barclay, *A New Testament Wordbook;* George Burnaby, *Christian Words and Christian Meanings;* Albert N. Williams, *Key Words of the Bible;* Adam Fox, *Meet the Greek Testament;* Norman H. Snaith, *The Distinctive Ideas of the Old Testament;* and a special section on word study in Ernest D. Burton, *The Epistle to the Galatians,* in the International Critical Commentary series. Good Bible dictionaries are also fruitful sources of word study. There are other works of a similar nature coming from the press from time to time, for which the pastor should be constantly on the lookout.

The fourth source of information as to word meanings is the standard commentaries which are based on the original languages. Frequently Luther or Calvin or Johann Bengel gives a description of word content which is astonishingly clear and up-to-date. Besides such classics as these, many modern commentaries prove fruitful in this regard. Ministers with limited budgets should avoid spending money on books of modern sermons and direct homiletic helps, and should through the years concentrate on building a library of the best commentaries.

Two further areas of study should be checked, if possible. The discovery of the Papyri served to indicate that the New Testament was not written in a special "language of the Holy Ghost," but in the popular speech of the common man of the first-century Greco-Roman world. There are times when Papyri usage throws a good deal of light on word meanings. The most fruitful source of study in this regard is James Moulton and George Milligan's *Vocabulary of the Greek Testament,* where many New Testament words are listed and examples of their use in the Papyri given. If the student desires to roam further into this area, he should consult such works as Gustav Adolf Deissmann's *Light from the Ancient East* and *Bible Studies,* George Milligan's *Here and There Among the Papyri,* and E. D. Head's *New Testament Life and Literature as Reflected in the Papyri.*

Perhaps more fruitful than the Papyri is the light thrown on New Testament words by the Septuagint. The writers of the New Testament were profound students of the Old Testament. Their usage of Greek words, therefore, was more often based on the meanings which had flowed into those words from the Old Testament than on the usage of the pagan world around them. It has become increasingly clear, therefore, that the Septuagint is a fruitful tool in helping to determine the theological significance of words in the New Testament. The standard aid at this point is Edwin Hatch and Henry Redpath's *Concordance to the Septuagint.* It is unfortunate that this work is so expensive and that so few copies are available. The best that the average student may hope for is to be near enough a good theological library to avail himself of this work for reference purposes. It is to be hoped that before long someone will publish a cheap edition of a concordance to the Septuagint, which would measurably enrich the study of the Bible for ministers.

But words alone are not language. They are put in combination. Phrases, clauses, sentences, combine words into speech. The next step, therefore, after coming to grips with word meanings, is to turn to syntax, the study of words in combination. Perhaps the first stage in this process is to parse the sentence or sentences with which one is dealing. This may be done by reducing the sentence to its simplest form—its subject and main verb, then trying to arrange the qualifying words, phrases, clauses, around this central core, in order to examine what their relationship to it is and what each contributes to an understanding of the writer's thought.

Two things, among others, will call for special attention here. The first is the force of prepositions. Archibald T. Robertson's little book *The Minister and His Greek New Testament* has a chapter in it entitled "Pictures in Prepositions." This is a fruitful example of how the force of prepositions often throws great light on what was stirring in the mind and heart of an author and yields up valuable grist for the homiletical mill. The second is the function of tenses. This is particularly fruitful in the study of the New Testament, where the force of Greek tenses is very revealing.

Syntactical matters can be examined fruitfully by those who are not experts in the language through consulting good reference grammars. These are often thoroughly indexed by scripture passages, and a quick check of each reference to the passage under consideration may yield up exactly what one is looking for. Beyond that, grammars are indexed by subjects which aid in tracing down exact information. Even if one is not adept at identifying forms in the original languages, he may determine what they are by the use of Bagster's *Analytical Greek Lexicon* for the New Testament and *The Analytical Hebrew and Chaldee Lexicon* for the Old Testament. These works list and identify every word used in the Bible. Armed with the information which these give about forms, the function of each form may then be checked in such reference grammars as A. T. Robertson's *Grammar of the Greek New Testament in the Light of Historical Research,* or Harvey Dana and Julius Mantey's *Manual Grammar of the Greek New Testament,* or James Hope

Moulton's *Grammar of New Testament Greek,* or A. E. Cowley's translation of Kautzsch's edition of *Gesenius' Hebrew Grammar.*

With such preparation as this behind him, the minister is now ready to begin to work directly toward his sermon. He may, in the light of this linguistic and grammatical study, go back and read the passage in the English several times, in order to co-ordinate the information he has found with the flowing sweep of thought of the larger passage. He may then want to make a list of all the truths he has discovered in his study, bringing together the jottings he has no doubt been making through all the process and distilling from them the most worthy results. Then he will ask himself which of these truths is central to the thought of the passage. This may become his theme. Or if he chooses to preach on one of the subsidiary themes, he will seek to set it in its relation to the central theme and develop it in his sermon as it is controlled by the major drive of the passage. A search should then be made for the elements of balance in the passage, which preserve the truth in its wholeness and help to avoid the peril of falsehood through exaggeration. The next step will be to ask what the other truths in the passage have to say about the theme on which the sermon is to be preached. This will determine the development of thought in the sermon. All of these steps, however, will be taken in the light of a clearly defined aim, an aim consonant with the purpose for which the scriptural passage was originally called forth. The final form of the sermon should seek to convey the emotional mood of the passage on which it is based, in the hope of touching thought with emotion which will lead to action. Each of these specific elements which go into the making of a truly biblical sermon will be dealt with in succeeding chapters.

With all these facets of preparation behind him, the minister's own individuality will determine his final treatment of the scripture on which his sermon is based. There is room for infinite variety here. Exposition does not demand any particular form. It demands only that the content of the message be the outgrowth of the study of the Scriptures. Beyond that, all the resources of individual genius may be brought to play on this message, so that its presentation will be as manifold in form as the personality and gifts of ministers are manifold. The whole of one's theological understanding, his knowledge of life and men and books, his grasp of history, his understanding of the currents which flow through contemporary life, will be brought to the service of the Scriptures in an effort to phrase their truth in a way that is both relevant and convincing. The creative impulses of each man, however, will be moving firmly within the control of the thought of the biblical writers, and the message will not be his in the sense that he has originated it, but only in the sense that he has appropriated, through ardent study, the message of prophet and apostle. Archbishop Whately once remarked that prophets and apostles can preach better than we can! It is our job to let them speak through us, so that the God who spoke uniquely through them may speak his living word through us in our time.

It will readily be seen that such a process as described above can hardly be done on the run or in a hurried session in the study on Saturday night. To be faithful to some such process as this, however, will become easier as time goes by. Stages in the process may be combined. Knowledge that is gleaned through preparation for one sermon will bear fruit in another. One's preaching will grow in fullness and depth, and he will be sustained by the confidence that he has at least made an honest effort to help answer the prayer of Augustine: "O let thy Scriptures be my pure delight, let me not be deceived in them, neither let me deceive by them."

III

DETERMINING THE CONTENT

Theme

———•———

Any sermon worthy of the name should have a theme. Ideally, any single sermon should have just one major idea. The points or subdivisions should be parts of this one grand thought. Just as bites of any particular food are all parts of the whole, cut into sizes that are both palatable and digestible, so the points of a sermon should be smaller sections of the one theme, broken into tinier fragments so that the mind may grasp them and the life assimilate them. Two or three or four points which are not parts of one great idea do not make a sermon—they are two or three or four sermons all preached on one occasion. Scattered comments on a biblical passage do not constitute a sermon. "Good commentary is bullion; good exposition, coin." Before thought can be negotiable on the market of the mind, or before it can become food for the soul, it must be prepared in an orderly fashion so that it can be readily passed over from the preacher's mind and heart to the minds and hearts of others.

A sermon should be a bullet, not bird shot. It ought to be designed to hit the hearer in one vital spot, rather than to spray him with scattered theological ideas unrelated to each other which touch him mildly in a dozen places. A sermon is synthesis, not analysis. The various thoughts of a passage must be broken down and studied in their interrelations in the minister's workshop, but these must be put together again and brought into the pulpit organized around a single center. The listener to a good sermon ought to go away from the service with one single impression; he should carry away a new grasp of one single phase of truth. Unity should be an outstanding characteristic of every good sermon. An intelligent listener should be able to rephrase the preacher's central thought in one sentence.

But how does one find this unifying theme when dealing with passages of scripture which themselves are very complex? Is it possible to disentangle from the maze of detail in most scripture passages a centralizing core around which everything else is focused? We may answer, in the main, "Yes." There are, of course, areas of scripture, such as the Proverbs, where a multitude of separate ideas are strung together like unmatched beads on a string. But for the most part, the Scriptures are made up of literary forms which involve interrelations of thought. These normally are linked together by some cohesive idea to which everything else is related. Stout phrased this aptly when he said:

This centralizing idea may be found in the conclusion of some assent-compelling argument; or in the highlight of some incident which has been described with all the charm of a masterpiece of word-painting; or in the occasion which leads up to some narrative or parable—occasion and narrative, or occasion and parable, being essential to each other in the proper understanding of the record. But in whatever form it may appear,—whether in these, or in any other—it is this centralizing element which is the key to the meaning of all the details of the passage. About this they gather. From this they develop. Without this they would not have been recorded.

The first and basic task in preparing a sermon, therefore, is to determine the theme of the passage of scripture on which it is to be based. This does not necessarily mean that this task is chronologically earliest in the process of study, for it may be that prolonged study is necessary before the exact theme of a passage may be discovered. But at whatever stage in the process of study the theme is discovered, it must at least be determined before the structure of the sermon itself may be determined. For how can one begin specific work on the structure of a sermon before he knows the basic idea around which it is to be built? If a sermon were the mere stringing together of religious thoughts, then the central theme of the passage of scripture on which it was allegedly based would be of little consequence. But the sermon would likewise be of little consequence.

We are now ready to state in simplest terms the burden of this chapter. It is this: *Every sermon should have a theme, and that theme should be the theme of the portion of Scripture on which it is based.* On first hearing, this sounds unimpressive and *elementary.* It seems almost as needless as saying that the way to walk is to take balanced steps or that the way to eat is to bite, chew, and swallow. The justification for pressing such a naïve and pedestrian principle lies in the simple fact that, basic though it is, it is frequently honored in the breach more than in the observance by a large number of preachers. And those who fail to make the theme of their sermons that of the passage on which they are preaching are not only the poorly trained clergy of the minor sects, nor only the few men of one talent who could not be expected to do better, but also highly trained ministers of influential pulpits—men whose learning and ability are beyond question. Apparently there has either been a fault in ministerial training, or the average minister prefers to take the easy way of allegedly preaching on texts whose central meaning he has not taken the trouble to discover.

Perhaps the best way to see this clearly is to set before us some illustrations of what is actually being done in modern pulpits with regard to sermon themes. Examples may sharpen what otherwise might be questioned. A few years ago a sermon appeared in a religious magazine entitled "The Challenge of the Christian Home." The theme was that "the secret of a happy home"—a lost secret in our time because of the tragic breakdown of family life—is "the recognition that the home is a two-way proposition. It involves the responsibility of both parents and children." This theme was then developed in the following way:

I. The responsibility of the parents—these are fourfold:
    A. To teach our children to live acceptably in society.
    B. To set our children an example.
    C. Discipline.
    D. Patience.

II. The responsibility of children—these are threefold:
    A. Recognition that parents are seeking their welfare.
    B. Appreciation of what parents do for them.
    C. Co-operation with their parents.

Now what was the text on which all this was allegedly based? It was a passage in Isa. 39:4: "What have they seen in your house?" A casual glance at the passage in Isaiah indicates that this question was addressed to King Hezekiah by the prophet immediately after a diplomatic visit from envoys of Merodach-baladan, son of the king of Babylon. When Isaiah addressed to him the question, "What have they seen in your house?" he had no reference whatsoever to the home life of Hezekiah. He was rather asking what military information Hezekiah had given to the Babylonian envoys. This becomes unmistakably clear in Hezekiah's reply: "They have seen all that is in my house; there is nothing in my storehouses that I did not show them." This is further reinforced by an earlier word which says that "Hezekiah welcomed them; and he showed them his treasure house, the silver, the gold, the spices, the precious oil, his whole armory, all that was found in his storehouses. There was nothing in his house or in all his realm that Hezekiah did not show them." From these words, it is quite plain that the word "house" had not the remotest relationship to Hezekiah's family life—nor, incidentally, to ours—but was rather a term describing the military resources of the king.

At that time both Babylon and Judah were in the control of the Assyrians. Under Merodach-baladan, Babylon had revolted and for a period had a taste of freedom. Her desire was to stir other vassal states of Assyria to revolt, in the hope that by concerted action they might all gain permanent freedom, or at least Babylon might maintain her independence because of the trouble brewing elsewhere in the Assyrian empire. Merodach, therefore, sent an embassy to Hezekiah ostensibly to congratulate him on his recovery to health after a serious illness, but with the secret mission of finding out how much military strength Hezekiah might provide for a concerted effort to overthrow Assyrian suzerainty. Isaiah had counseled formerly against trust in military alliances for Judah and had insisted that Judah's future was assured only through faith in God. But although he had opposed an alliance with Assyria, he insisted that the alliance having been made, it should be honored. Now, in the planned revolt against Assyria at the behest of Merodach, Judah was merely adding sin to sin. If there was to be any way out of the plight caused by former infidelity to God, it would be a deliverance wrought by God in his mercy, and not by political duplicity and human cleverness. After the Babylonian envoys have returned, therefore, the prophet comes to find out whether the king had accepted his counsel or whether he had abandoned faith for alliances. When Hezekiah admits that he had shown the messengers from Babylon all his resources, implying that he was at that time minded to enter a military alliance against Assyria, Isaiah replied: "Hear the word of the Lord of hosts: Behold, the days are coming, when all that is in your house, and that which your fathers have stored up till this day, shall be carried to Babylon; nothing shall be left, says the Lord." The prophet saw clearly that the nation's refusal to trust in God, dramatized in the behavior of the king, would ultimately lead to judgment through captivity.

This passage is a marvelous one to set forth obedience to, and faith in, the purpose of God rather than trust in clever diplomacy. The theme could be enriched by drawing upon the surrounding materials. Hezekiah had dramatically witnessed in his own personal experience what the prophet was talking about for the whole nation. He had faced an enemy worse than the Assyrian—death. And in this crisis, where no human resolution or resources could avail, God had intervened in his behalf and raised him up. But this raising up was not merely for his own sake. It was a sign that God intended to use him as the instrument of saving the nation.

Isaiah was commanded to say to him: "I will add fifteen years to your life. I will deliver you and this city out of the hand of the king of Assyria, and defend this city" (Isa. 38:5-6). Here God had shown in unmistakable and dramatic terms that he was hovering over the nation to protect it. But shortly thereafter, in defiance of the word of the Lord through the prophet, in forgetfulness of God's deliverance from death, and in trust in his own cleverness in diplomacy, Hezekiah had offered to join in a military coalition with a pagan power, in order to insure the nation's survival. He forgot that the God who had shown himself Lord of death was also Lord of history. He succumbed to a policy of nation-building without God and was unmindful of the truth which his religious heritage and his own experience should have confirmed, that "unless the Lord builds the house, those who build it labor in vain. Unless the Lord watches over the city, the watchman stays awake in vain" (Ps. 127:1).

There is truth here for every generation to recapture. But it has no bearing whatsoever on home life, either ancient or modern. To preach on the Christian home with it as a basis is to miss entirely the theme of the passage. This is a good example of a so-called topical sermon which is in no sense expository. Neither theme nor points are drawn from the Scriptures, and the development of the sermon is introduced by the formula, "As I see it. . . ." It is a devotional lecture, setting forth some ideas of the minister on the sort of homes we should have. It is a good lecture, but dare we call it a sermon?

Another striking example of missing the theme of a passage appeared some years ago in a religious magazine which claims to be the herald of strict loyalty to the Scriptures and the literary spearhead of a twentieth-century Reformation. It has the word "beacon" in its title, with the seeming implication that it is one of the very few, if not the only, beacon lights of truth left to shine into the darkness of this old world. It is the "beacon" which sits atop the "impregnable rock of Holy Scripture" to throw light on what the Bible means. On the occasion to which I refer, the birthday of this religious journal was being celebrated at a banquet. The speaker of the evening presented what must have been, to his mind, the biblical basis of the journal's name. He used as his text, Isa. 30:17: "Till ye be left as a beacon upon the top of a mountain, and as an ensign on a hill." (A.S.V.) I did not hear the address, so I cannot vouch for its content. But since it was an address in celebration of the birthday of the *Beacon,* and since while the speaker spoke, a revolving beacon light atop a seven-foot steel structure on a nearby table beamed its light to the listeners, it would not seem unfair to assume that the address had some bearing on the mission of the journal whose birthday was being celebrated. If this be true, then it is quite likely that the address of the evening missed the theme of the passage of scripture on which it was allegedly based.

In the Isaiah passage the prophet is speaking a strong word of rebuke to Judah. God has offered them sanctuary in the tenderest terms. "In returning and rest shall ye be saved; in quietness and in confidence shall be your strength." But was Judah willing quietly to place her confidence in God and await his deliverance? "No!" said they, "We will flee upon horses. . . . We will ride upon the swift." But, says the prophet, your pursuers will also be swift. The end result will be so disconcerting that Judah's courage will entirely disappear, and they will become so demoralized that "one thousand shall flee at the threat of one; at the threat of five you shall flee: till ye be left as a beacon upon the top of a mountain, and as an ensign on a hill." The point is that there will be no place to flee for refuge, no place to hide from the justice of the Almighty whose grace they had refused. They will be as assailable as a lone beacon on a mountaintop, with no possible defense in sight. There may have been a more profound bearing on the subject of the evening than the speaker knew, but had the theme of the scripture passage been clearly applied, it would no doubt measurably have robbed the evening of some of its joy!

But quite apart from these extreme instances of glaring misinterpretation, there are many occasions when a minister who has made an honest effort to relate the theme of his sermon to that of his passage, may be trapped into a subtle deviation of which he is not aware. Sometimes the theme of a passage is reflected in a sermon in such a general way that sermon and passage are not really brought together into any vital relationship. An example of this is to be seen in a sermon based on Paul's words in Eph. 5:25-27: "Christ also loved the church,

and gave himself for it; . . . that he might present it to himself
a glorious church." (K.J.V.) The sermon begins: "What did
the apostle mean by the words, 'a glorious church'? He does
not say exactly. Let me mention a few of the things which that
phrase means to me." The development then continues with
no further reference to the thought of Paul whatsoever. In this
instance, the theme of the sermon seems to parallel the theme
of the passage. "A glorious church" is the theme of both. But
since the sermon does not develop the idea of a glorious church
in the same terms that the passage does, the relationship is purely
accidental and unreal. Why use a text from Paul if the sermon
is not to set forth what Paul had to say?

It may be difficult to know exactly what Paul had in mind
by the phrase "a glorious church," but there are a good many
hints in the larger passage from which these words come which
might serve as clues. Paul speaks of the church being "sancti-
fied" by Christ; he describes the church as having been
"cleansed" by the "washing of water by the word"; he elaborates
the term "glorious" by the use of the words without "spot, or
wrinkle, or any such thing"; and ends with the thought that the
church might "be holy and without blemish." These may be
terms difficult to define, but the use of the best resources of
biblical study could certainly aid in setting them in the general
context of Pauline thought. Then, too, there is a tremendous
Christian dynamic behind all this in the fact that "Christ also
loved the church, and gave himself up for it," which might
have lifted the sermon above the level of mere human advice and
ministerial urging and given it a cutting edge that had a dis-
tinctly New Testament quality.

Furthermore, the sermon had in it the note of social passion,
which might have been greatly undergirded by the fact that
the text is rooted in a long passage on the ideal relation between husbands and wives in the Christian faith, which "one-

ness" is more than suggestive of the oneness that should exist between the members of the body of Christ and between Christians and Christ in sharing our Lord's concern for the world. All that the preacher had in mind to say—and more—was right in the passage, where it might have been reinforced with the weight of biblical authority and with the dynamic of the Pauline evangel. Had the theme of the sermon paralleled that of the passage not only in the superficial sense that they both spoke of a "glorious" church, but also in the deeper sense that the sermon had conveyed what Paul was trying to say about a "glorious" church, then the sermon would have been truly biblical and, in the judgment of the writer, measurably strengthened.

Another example presents an even more subtle failure to capture the theme of a passage. Taking his text from the story of the Transfiguration in Matt. 17:7, where Jesus touched the fallen disciples and said, "Rise, and have no fear," a leading minister preached on the theme, "Christ's Cure for Fear." The successive points were:

> I. Christ's cure for physical fear. Since the physical hazards of a mechanical age are greatly increased, we need more than ever Christ's release from physical fear.

> II. Christ's cure for mental fear. The stresses of these complex times have increased tenfold over those of former periods of history, making Christ's mastery of mental fears the more imperative.

> III. Christ's cure for social and economic fears. The disparities and rivalries in modern society are such that no other than Christ can overcome them.

Now, on the surface it looks as though the theme of this sermon were the theme of the passage from which it was preached. Christ said to the ancient disciples, "Rise, and have no fear." He says the same to modern men, cursed by the manifold manifestations of personal and social fears in our time. But a more careful examination of the passage from which the text is taken reveals that the theme of the sermon was quite other than the theme of the passage. The fear with which the disciples were overcome had nothing to do with physical, mental, social, and economic fears. And when Jesus said to them, "Rise, and have no fear," he did not mean, "Rise and face life courageously, no matter how many the dangers to your body life entails, no matter how great the possibility of mental strain, or how much you may seem to be victimized by social and economic forces over which you have no control." No doubt Christ does say this, but it cannot justly be deduced from this passage.

The fear from which the disciples were suffering at that moment is the type of fear for which modern man seems to have lost the capacity. They had seen the glory of God until they were struck down! They were so overcome with a sense of the transcendent majesty of the divine that they recoiled in desperate awe. They experienced something of what their own Scriptures depicted when God replied to Moses' request to see His glory, "You cannot see my face; for man shall not see me and live." They felt something of what Jacob experienced when, after a face-to-face encounter with God at Peniel, he exclaimed, "I have seen God face to face, and yet my life is preserved!" They were touched with something of the sublime reverence with which Isaiah cried out when he saw the Lord, "Woe is me! For I am lost; . . . for my eyes have seen the King, the Lord of hosts!" They felt what the Revelator must have felt when he saw "one like a son of man, . . . his head and his hair were white as white wool, white as snow; his eyes were like a flame of fire, his feet were like burnished bronze, . . . his voice was like the sound of many waters; . . . from his mouth issued a sharp two-edged sword, and his face was like the sun shining in full strength." How did the Revelator respond to this sight of the Son of man? "When I saw him," he writes, "I fell at his feet as though dead." It was this reverential awe, this human recoil of sinful man from the awful holiness of God, which struck the disciples to the ground on the Transfiguration mount.

And Christ's cure for that kind of fear lies in the fact that he is the Son of God, with whom the Father was well pleased, who took upon himself the role of the Suffering Servant and fulfilled all righteousness, bringing to a completion both the Law and the prophets and destroying man's last enemy—death. He has the cure for man's fear of a holy God because he can lay "his right hand" upon us and say, "Fear not, I am the first and the last, and the living one; I died, and behold I am alive for evermore, and I have the keys of Death and Hades." The voice from the cloud says, "Listen to him." It is as we hear his word of judgment and cry out with Peter, "Depart from me, for I am a sinful man, O Lord," and then listen to Him say, "Fear not, I am the first and the last, and the living one; . . . I have the keys of Death and Hades," that we shall know His cure for fear at a deeper level than our physical, mental, and social fears.

A sermon justly based on this text would necessarily move somewhere along this general line of thought, for this is the direction in which the thought of the passage is moving. To use this text to preach on fear in general, rather than on the reverential awe of sinful man in the presence of God's glory, and to preach a sermon on it which makes no effort whatsoever to interpret it in the light of the disciples' experience on the Mount of Transfiguration, is to miss the theme of the passage and to violate one of the basic principles of true biblical preaching—

that the theme of the sermon should be the theme of the passage on which it is based.

Another example indicates how a "textual" sermon, based on a word of scripture divorced from its setting, may present a theme allegedly based on the Word of God but in reality flying full in the face of that Word. A text frequently used, to which Calvin Coolidge as president once made historic reference in the interests of bolstering his conception of statecraft, is found in Ps. 11:3: "If the foundations are destroyed, what can the righteous do?" From this text has been preached many a sermon, the burden of whose thought was that we must rebuild the foundations of life or the righteous will have no place on which to stand, and society is certain to collapse. Although this may be a truth, in fact it may be a biblical truth, yet it has not the remotest connection with the thought of these words in the psalm. These words are neither a word of God nor of the psalmist. They are rather the word of the devil spoken through a cynic whose faith had quailed. They are a part of the advice of an enemy of faith, of a timid soul who is cynically despondent, who has given up hope, who is unable to see any reason why righteous men should make any further effort at all. The implication of the cynical statement is that since the foundations have been destroyed, the righteous can do nothing. Therefore, "flee" is the word. Give up, and quit!

The psalmist, however, is not thus minded. He has opened the psalm with the words: "In the Lord I take refuge; how can you say to me, 'Flee like a bird to the mountains . . .'?" And he continues: "The Lord is in his holy temple, the Lord's throne is in heaven." The foundations may look as though they were crumbling to men who have no eyes of faith, but the believer sees that which is invisible. He sees that the Lord is still in control of affairs, that the foundations of his heavenly throne stand sure. In the light of this faith, therefore, he refuses the advice of the cynic who is ready to quit, and he counters that there is still much that the righteous man can do.

What Can the Righteous Do?

I. The righteous can *still believe in God.* "In the Lord I take refuge," cries the psalmist. "The Lord is in his holy temple, the Lord's throne is in heaven." The foundations of society as we know it may be crumbling, but not the foundations of the universe. Look beyond, therefore, with the eyes of faith, to eternal foundations which, when all is shaken that can be shaken, remain.

II. The righteous can *keep on being righteous.* He can continue to pursue simple goodness. He can keep the inner citadel of the soul clean and wholesome in the sight of Him whose "eyes behold . . . the children of men. The Lord tests the righteous and the wicked, and his soul hates him that loves violence."

III. The righteous can *maintain a sense of divine companionship.* "The upright shall behold his face," says the psalmist. This is a biblical expression meaning to have fellowship with another, to have free access into the presence of another. Ultimately, says the writer of the Revelation, "his servants shall worship him; they shall see his face." Until then, we may now see the "light of the knowledge of the glory of God in the face of Jesus Christ," a light which may be for us "a dawning light which shines more and more unto the perfect day."

One further example of how the larger relations of a passage determine its theme may be seen in Ps. 69:6, in which the psalmist cries out: "Let not those who hope in thee be put to shame through me, O Lord God of hosts; let not those who seek thee be brought to dishonor through me, O God of Israel." On first reading these words they sound like the prayer of a penitent man asking that his own personal sins shall not stand in the way of others getting to God. Who of us has not known the devastating backwash of his own sin, which having turned to ashes for him, is now plainly seen as a betrayal of the faith and an impediment in the way of others getting to God? The awakening awareness of the social responsibility of one's sin is one of the most devastating experiences that can come to a man, and one which makes him cry out with deep feeling, "Let not those who seek thee be brought to dishonor through me."

But this is neither the thought nor the mood of these words in this psalm. Here is a man who, rather than being disloyal to his God, has been "consumed" with zeal for God's house. He is one who has been so concerned about the interests of God that he can say to the Almighty without any sense of self-commendation: "The insults of those who insult thee have fallen on me." Here is a transparent soul who has made God the passion of his life and has paid dearly for it. He has been a byword to the crowd who sit gossiping at the city gate. Drunkards have made up bawdy songs about him. He has known reproach, shame, dishonor, insults. He has known the utter loneliness of a soul who looked for one sympathetic friend and found him not. "I looked for pity, but there was none; and for comforters, but I found none."

The fear of the psalmist now is that through what has happened to him, others may be deterred from the path of loyalty to God. They may look at him and say, "Well, if that is what happens to a man zealous for God, it will be better either to be wicked, or at least to maintain an attitude of strict neutrality toward spiritual issues." The psalmist pleads that his sufferings shall not deter other men from loyalty to the right. To have one's sufferings for righteousness deter others from loyalty to the right and to find one's commitment to God driving others away from Him, must come very close to plumbing the depths of spiritual agony.

Is it any wonder that all four of the New Testament evangelists saw a connection between this psalm and the experience of Jesus on the Cross? The desolation which the soul knows when even suffering does not excite pity and when bystanders offer vinegar to a man who cries out, "I thirst," was a part of Jesus' experience of walking the lonely path of commitment to God. And it was Jesus' very goodness which made other men turn their backs upon God. "If I had not come and spoken to them," he said in the Fourth Gospel, "they would not have sin; . . . If I had not done among them the works which no one else did, they would not have sin; but now they have seen and hated both me and my Father." Then he interprets the meaning of his own experience in the light of Ps. 69, when he continues: "It is to fulfil the word that is written in their law, 'They hated me without a cause.'"

Add to this the fact that the early church interpreted the meaning of the cleansing of the Temple in this same light, finding their clue to it in this sixty-ninth psalm, in the words, "Zeal for thy house will consume me." They saw something of the struggle in Jesus' soul when his coming into the world meant the destruction of the very Judaism he had come to save. They sensed something of the unimaginable pathos in the soul of Jesus which foresaw the destruction of the temple which had been forty-six years in building at that time and which, along with the law and priesthood and sacrificial system there carried on, was all that Judaism had left from her heritage through

Abraham, Moses, and David. To turn God's people away from God by his own zealous commitment to God must have been to Jesus one of the bitterest elements of the Cross.

And yet, if the pathos of Ps. 69 found its counterpart in the experience of Jesus, so must its final note of triumphant confidence have brought him strength. For the psalm ends with the fact that spiritual devotion exceeds all ceremonial religion and calls on heaven and earth to praise God for the fact that he "will save Zion and rebuild the cities of Judah; and his servants . . . and those who love his name shall dwell in it." It is little wonder, then, that Ps. 69 bulks so largely in the New Testament. In a profound sense, it is a Christological psalm, linking Old and New Testaments and bringing the best in Israel to a transcendent fulfillment in Jesus. It is in this direction that the thought of a sermon based on this psalm will move if its theme is that of the ancient Scripture.

While we are discussing the question of theme, it will suffice to give one brief word about poetic license which is a travesty on scripture. No doubt there has been more than one preacher —I know that there was one—who has preached eloquently from Matt. 24:20 in moving terms which have been appealing to the hearers, but which have been nothing other than sheer poetic fancy. The text is, "Pray that your flight may not be in winter." The theme—"Do not delay coming to Christ until age has set the grooves of life so deeply that one cannot get out of them!" Flee to Jesus in the springtime of life, not in life's winter! Well, had the minister used even the entire verse, he might have spared himself this ludicrous play on words. The full verse reads, "Pray that your flight may not be in winter *or on a sabbath.*" Unless one could grow suddenly old between sabbaths, the advantages of coming to Christ in youth can hardly be drawn from this text! The winter in this passage is quite literal and not poetic, and to use scripture in this poetic fashion is, though the preacher did not mean it so, to display an irreverence for the Word of God and to turn Holy Scripture into a pious volume of fairy tales or a religious *Alice in Wonderland*.

There is yet one question concerning the theme of a sermon which must be faced. We have been insisting that a truly biblical sermon is one whose theme is the theme of the passage on which it is based. But do not many passages of scripture have more than one theme? Obviously they do. It is of the nature of literature to combine thoughts and to incorporate into a living whole a complex range of ideas. The Bible has this in common with all great literature. In dealing with a passage which brings together a wide range of truths, the preacher must ask himself the question: "Which of these can rightly be the theme of a sermon based on this scripture?" The answer is that any one of the themes in a passage may justly be central in a sermon. In the study of the passage, however, the major theme should first be discovered and the relation of the subsidiary themes to the major theme clearly envisioned in the mind of the preacher. Then, if one of the secondary themes becomes the theme of the sermon it should be developed in such a fashion that its relation to the major theme will clearly be seen.

For example, several very important Christian truths are to be found in I Pet. 1:17-21. "And if you invoke as Father"— there is the fatherhood of God. "You know that you were ransomed . . . not with perishable things such as silver or gold, but with the precious blood of Christ"—there is the atonement. "A lamb without blemish or spot"—there is the perfection of Christ. "Through him you have confidence in God"—there is the intimate relation of Christ to the believer. "Who raised him from the dead and gave him glory"—there is the resurrection and ascension and session at God's right hand. Now any one of these themes may legitimately be used from this passage as the basis of a true expository sermon. But should any one of them be chosen, it cannot justly be developed without first discovering the major theme which the apostle had in mind when he penned these words, and then developing it in its relation to that major theme.

What is the drive of the entire passage? Why were these subsidiary ideas introduced into the total sweep of the apostle's message here? The answer is plainly to be found in an analysis of the entire thought development of verses 13-25. Verse 13 begins with the word "therefore," which is a signpost pointing back to what has already been developed. In verses 3-12 the apostle has been setting forth in lofty terms his conception of the salvation which is ours through the gospel. This glorious salvation, he insists, has certain implications for life for all those who believe it. The "therefore" of verse 13 introduces these implications which are set forth in the form of four great imperatives —all put in the strong aorist imperative tense, which is designed to go beyond mere advice and to lay upon the reader the burden of inescapable obligation. The gospel issues in life in at least four ways, says the writer. If you believe the "good news" of salvation, then:

    I. "Hope."

    II. "Be holy . . . in all your conduct."

    III. "Conduct yourselves with fear."

    IV. "Love one another earnestly."

Now all the truths mentioned above are related to the third of these imperatives—"Conduct yourselves with fear throughout the time of your exile." They are all introduced into the passage to undergird this great life imperative.

If, then, the fatherhood of God becomes the theme of a sermon from this passage, it should be developed from the standpoint of its bearing on the translation into life of the reverential awe and holy seriousness engendered by a filial relation to the Father "who judges each one impartially according to his deeds." Should one preach from this passage on the atonement, it would not be a mere general approach to this great subject, but a definite unfolding of the bearing of the costliness of our redemption on a life mood of reverential fear toward God and man. If the perfection of Christ's holiness, or the intimate relation of Christ to the believer, or the Resurrection and Ascension, be the theme of a sermon from this passage, they likewise should be approached through their bearing on the filial awe which should characterize the total life of a believer. Any theme of a scripture passage may form the basis for an expository sermon, if the sermon truly reflects the interrelations of the particular theme with the major sweep of thought of which it is a part.

Another instance of the control of the minor themes of a passage by the major theme may be seen in the glorious climax of Paul's argument in the Epistle to the Romans, chapter 8, verses 28-39. This, one of the greatest passages Paul ever penned, is bristling with themes. And what is more, many of them are the foundational truths on which the faith is built. Now, should one preach from this great section, which of the truths could properly be the theme of a sermon?

It might be well to list just a few of the major doctrines here mentioned:

    I. The love of God.
        A. "The love of Christ."
        B. "The love of God in Christ Jesus our Lord."

II. The atonement.

    A. "He who did not spare his own Son but gave him up for us all."

    B. "Christ Jesus, who died."

III. Providence.

    A. "In everything God works for good with those who love him."

    B. "For those whom he foreknew he also predestined."

    C. "Will he not also give us all things with him?"

IV. The deity of Christ.

    "His own Son."

V. The security of the believer.

    A. "We know that in everything God works for good with those who love him."

    B. "It is God who justifies; who is to condemn?"

    C. "Who shall separate us from the love of Christ?"

    D. "In all these things we are more than conquerors."

    E. "For I am sure that . . . [nothing] . . . will be able to separate us."

Besides these, there are countless other themes in this great passage.

Now which of these themes should rightly be used as the basis for an exposition of this passage? The answer is, any one of them. But before any particular theme could so be presented in order justly to reflect the drive of Paul's thought here, a decision would have to be made as to which of these themes is central, so that the subsidiary themes could be developed in their relation to the major theme.

The terminology of the passage, as well as its structure, suggests that the focus of Paul's thought here is *the security of the believer.* The passage opens with the words "we know" and closes with the affirmation "I am sure." The materials brought in between these two declarations of certainty abound in expressions which indicate that the major theme here is that the believer is so secure in God's love that nothing in heaven or earth, in time or eternity, can ever shake that security. If, therefore, one should choose to make one of the subsidiary themes focal in a sermon, he should try to develop that theme in its relation to the believer's security.

One could well preach on the atonement from this passage. His sermon, however, should not be a mere general approach to that doctrine. It should rather present the atonement from the standpoint of its guarantee of the believer's security. God "did not spare his own Son but gave him up for us all"—this is the solid basis on which our persuasion rests that he will "also give us all things with him," and that nothing "in all creation, will be able to separate us from the love of God in Christ Jesus our Lord."

Or if one were to preach on the divine providence from this passage, his sermon should not be a theoretical argument designed to score a point in theology, but should be presented from the standpoint of its relation to the security of the believer in the adversities of life. All the way from "foreknew" to "glorified," the life of the believer is caught up in a beneficent purpose conceived in the heart of God and born out of his transcendent love manifested in Christ—shown clearly in his death and vindicated in his resurrection. On this the faith of the believer rests in times of "tribulation, or distress, or persecution, or famine, or nakedness, or peril, or sword." Paul is here not offering an abstract argument about predestination, but is digging around the foundations on which a believer's security rests. He is asking the suffering Christian to look with him once more at the solidity and unshakableness of these foundations, so that he may rest secure while the storms which cause him to fear do their worst.

There is a story of a town which maintained its existence through the output of several shoe factories, but in which none of the inhabitants wore shoes. A stranger once spent a long time inquiring of owners, workers, merchants, housewives, and town waifs why, in a town where shoes were made, nobody wore shoes. The only answer he could get from any of them was, "Why don't we?" We preachers claim to be interpreters of Holy Scripture. Our time is given to us for special study, so that we can delve more deeply into the meaning of revealed truth and seek, under the guidance and empowering of the Holy Spirit, to help others to grasp the truth and feel the throb of God's unique redemptive action in Christ set forth in the Bible. But why don't we make the themes of our sermons the themes of the passages on which they are based?

Why don't we?

IV

CREATING THE PROPORTION

Balance

———•———

The morning newspaper carries the story of a tragedy at sea in which thirty-seven lives, out of a crew of forty-eight, were lost when a cargo ship capsized. The eleven survivors reported that "it all happened faster than you could believe." The ship "sank so fast there was no time to send an SOS." What caused it? It was lack of balance. As the ship encountered high seas, suddenly the cargo of iron ore shifted, throwing the weight to one side and almost immediately capsizing the ship.

Lack of balance is a homiletical as well as a nautical danger. Many a sermon has been the victim of shifted cargo. To overweight truth on one side may not show up as dramatically as a capsized boat, but both homiletically and theologically it is equally disastrous. For half-truths may become untruths, if they are unrelated to other areas of truth which keep them in proper proportion and hold the ship of truth on an even keel.

Truth, by its very nature, is many-sided. The "simple" truth is seldom true. For in the realm of religion, the truth would necessarily correspond to the reality that is God, and the reality that is man, and the reality of the living relations in which God meets man. Since both God and man are in themselves very complex, and since the relationship between them is manifestly intricate, it is plain that religious truth is many-sided. It is equally plain that approaches to truth which take no account of this fullness and seek to force the whole range of truth through the narrow confines of one viewpoint, result in distortions which are to be both feared and shunned. Clarity in this field is not to be gained by the use of a telephoto lens, no matter how strong, which enlarges and makes plainer a narrow range of truth. What is needed is rather a wide-angle lens, which brings more of the landscape of reality within the range of our vision and enables us to set each facet of it in its proper relation to the larger whole.

This need is particularly felt in relation to some of the most profound elements of Christian truth. When we try to "think God's thoughts after him," they are too big to fit into the limits of our minds. Or when we think of truth as greater than God's "thought," as a living thing comprehending the approach of the redeeming God and the response of sinful man to him in faith, it is evident that however dynamic the personal encounter may be, it is something less than the sum total of successive encounters which recur through a lifetime of walking with God and much less than the sum total of divine encounters with the entire human race from Creation to the End.

Furthermore, there is always an element of unsolved mystery in the encounter of God with the human soul. The reverent believer who is confronted with God knows that he has experienced something the dimensions of which transcend all his thought or imagining, that he is in touch with a reality far greater than he can ever comprehend. The Bible abounds in expressions which confirm this. Listen to a few of them (K.J.V.): "passeth knowledge"; "passeth all understanding"; "joy unspeakable"; "the unsearchable riches of Christ"; "a great mystery"; "the mystery of iniquity"; "great is the mystery of godliness." All of these and kindred expressions remind us that when we think about him who "dwells in light inapproachable," we can only "see through a glass darkly" (K.J.V.). The mirror of finite minds is too small and too clouded to give a complete reflection of God or of the elements of his approach to the human soul.

The danger to which our limitations subject us is that we shall overstress partial phases of truth at the expense of other equally important aspects of it and send the ship of truth on its way badly listing or even capsize it altogether. Two areas of Christian truth in which this danger is particularly patent may serve to make the principle concrete. The first is the problem of the relation of the divine sovereignty to the freedom of the human will. Since the mind finds it difficult to come to rest in the presence of two seemingly irreconcilable truths, the tendency is to maintain one at the expense of the other, and so to overemphasize one that the other remains only as a way of speaking, without substance. Thus the divine sovereignty may become so focal in our thinking that man has no real freedom and is left as a puppet of the divine will in some sort of near approach to fatalism. Or, on the other hand, human freedom may loom so large in our thinking that God's will may become only his wish, his decisions are shorn of power, and the possibility stares us in the face that ultimately his purpose could be defeated by human rebellion. The former tends to make man just a toy of God, the latter tends to make God a prisoner of man.

A second area where lack of balance becomes a very concrete danger is in the realm of God's mighty action in redeeming men. The tendency here is to lay hold of some figure of redemption used in scripture and make that the only vehicle for expressing the atonement, to the exclusion of other equally valid figures of atonement set forth in the Bible. Sometimes the Bible speaks of atonement in terms of acquittal before a court of law. Sometimes it uses the figure of release from the bondage of slavery, God's victory in a conflict with an enemy who had enslaved man. At other times it is dealt with in the form of transfer of citizenship from one kingdom to another. At still other times atonement is pictured as the restoration of life from the dead. Again it is spoken of as the overcoming of personal alienation between man and God. Categories of the courts, the marketplace, the battlefield, the sacrificial offering, the family, are all summoned to the service of the doctrine of the atonement in the New Testament. And from these, theologians have developed the Ransom theory, the Satisfaction theory, the Substitutionary theory, the Governmental theory, the Moral Influence theory, the Mystical theory, and others, to try to give intellectual content to certain aspects of the biblical teaching on atonement. To make any one of these exhaustive to the exclusion of the others is to lose our sense of wholeness and to denude the doctrine of the atonement of some of its meaning and power.

John A. Hutton once remarked that when he found himself face to face with what looked like "irreconcilable alternatives," he tried to keep before his mind a principle laid down by Jesus in another connection: "What therefore God has joined together, let no man put asunder." Said Hutton: "There is always another side to the story. The great entertainment of Heaven for many a day will be, seeing the other side of a thousand things." A proper balance of emphasis on truth will seek to hold together the various insights of scripture which may seem to be mutually exclusive and will place only that stress on any one phase of truth which is commensurate with other features of the biblical revelation.

To adhere to this principle in the sermonic interpretation of scripture is asking no more than men are forced to do in other realms of endeavor. To take but one illustration from science, the theory of light has long been debated. What is light? One view was that light was the result of waves given off by the movement of electrons within the atom, visible light resulting from the motion of the outer electrons of the atom and invisible light resulting from the motion of the electrons nearer the nucleus. Many experiments were conducted on the basis of this hypothesis, with results which seemed to confirm the theory. On the other hand, the quantum theory, based on the researches of Max Planck and Albert Einstein, was advanced to explain light. According to this theory, light consists of little particles or bullets of energy, now called photons, which were atoms of energy, not matter. Experiments conducted on the basis of this hypothesis tended to confirm it and even to explain some phenomena which on the basis of the wave theory of light were inexplicable. At the same time, there were some proven elements of the behavior of light for which the wave theory accounted, but which the quantum theory left unexplained.

The impasse reached in the rivalry of these two theories was such that Sir William Bragg once remarked that if you should ask a creditable physicist to explain light, on Mondays, Wednesdays, and Fridays he would use the wave theory and on Tuesdays, Thursdays, and Saturdays the quantum theory. In both cases the physicist would have been right, but in neither case would he have been wholly right, for there is undoubted truth in both theories. Any balanced treatment of the theory of light, therefore, must reckon with these seemingly irreconcilable alternatives, and hold them together in its total explanation of light. This will remain permanently necessary until further advances are made in the study of light which enable scientists to construct a theory so transcending both of these that both are reconciled in the larger reality and the values of each are conserved. So in the realm of complementary but ir-reconcilable religious truths, they find their meeting place in the mind of God, where a larger understanding of truth brings into a glorious harmony all partial phases of reality. When we know as we are known, the perfect balance of opposite phases of reality will be plain.

The question of balance with relation to biblical preaching rests on two fundamental convictions. The first is that the Scriptures themselves are characterized by a delicacy of propor-tion which is one of the sure marks of their greatness. They are marked throughout by what John Ruskin called "the balance of harmonious opposites." Truth is interwoven with truth in such fashion that each holds the other in check and defines the limits within which it must be understood. This is done more often than not in subtle rather than in bold ways. But this is a mark of their excellence. "In bad compositions as in bad architecture," says Ruskin, "[balance] is formal, a tree on one side answering a tree on the other; but in good compositions, as in graceful statues, it is always easy, and sometimes hardly traceable." The biblical writers do not throw up glaring sign-posts nor call formal attention to what they are doing in main-taining proportion in their presentation of truth. They rather embody it in a "living symmetry" which needs no blatant trumpeter but which yields its secret to the painstaking gaze of a sensitive observer.

Let us take, as an example, the biblical handling of the doctrine of election, over which so many theological battles have been waged and about which so many extreme positions have been taken. To approach this doctrine from the stand-point of a logical rationale—either in the interests of establish-ing a dogma of "double predestination," which would exclude some men from the influences of God's love by God's choice, or of denying the validity of the doctrine by making of it a mere reflection of national or racial pride on the part of the Jews—is to do violence to the biblical presentation. And both of these overemphases have occurred, not only historically but also in modern times.

As I was writing these words there came in the mail a journal in which there was an article insisting on the divine election in terms of God's having chosen everything that happens. The writer even goes so far as to insist that "God in some sense is the cause of sin, for he is the sole ultimate cause of everything." He affirms that the Bible teaches this, but does not show where! On the other hand, one frequently runs across statements that the biblical doctrine of election is merely a reflection of the narrow nationalism and racial pride from which men like Jeremiah and Paul were never delivered. I have a vague remembrance that Hitler had something like this to say!

Now the Bible itself deals with election in terms quite other than either of these and always approaches it with a delicacy of balance which would spare the "enormities of interpretation" into which many have fallen, if they would but recognize it. The election of Israel is undoubtedly a central feature of the biblical revelation. Deut. 7:6 boldly declares: "The Lord your God has chosen you to be a people for his own possession, out of all the peoples that are on the face of the earth." Amos is in hearty agreement with this theology: "You only have I known of all the families of the earth" (3:2). Deutero-Isaiah speaks of "Jacob, whom I have chosen" (41:8). This theme is carried over into the New Testament. First Pet. 2:9 is typical when reference is made to the church as "a chosen race . . . God's own people." Even the Fourth Gospel, which is thought by some to be designed to overleap Jewish particularism and to universalize the gospel, bluntly affirms: "Salvation is from the Jews" (4:22).

If such passages as these are isolated, one might well conclude that they represent mere pride of race or national egotism. Other ancient peoples also claimed the elect favor of the gods, while modern theories of a super race or a super class are born of a consummate egotism which looks down on other men. But these passages in the Bible are not in isolation. They are set in relationship to other facets of truth. And when they are balanced over against these, the last thing that one could rightly conclude would be that they are expressive of arrogant bigotry. The Deuteronomist follows his affirmation of Israel's election with the humbling reminder: "It was not because you were more in number than any other people that the Lord set his love upon you and chose you, for you were the fewest of all peoples; but it is because the Lord loves you, and is keeping the oath which he swore to your fathers" (7: 7-8). This is surely not expressive of racial pride to be reminded that in themselves they were the most insignificant of all the peoples of the earth! Furthermore, the passage continues with a warning that this mighty love of God, so undeserved by them, laid on them an obligation to respond in obedience to God's will, and that the moment they forgot the obligation of obedience and became self-sufficient and proud, saying, "My power and the might of my hand," they would "surely perish" (8:17, 19).

The outcome of this is seen in the Amos passage: "You only have I known of all the families of the earth; *therefore* I will punish you for all your iniquities!" (3:2). God had not loved them because of any special excellence on their part, and when they failed to respond to God's undeserved favor, the end result was punishment. As Suzanne de Dietrich has said, "Election means a unique way of standing under God's judgment, not escaping that judgment." Contrast this with either ancient or modern racial or group pride which sits in judgment over others but never brings itself under judgment and never suspects its own sin, and one can readily see the balanced emphasis of the biblical writers.

As to the "enormities of interpretation" which have turned election into an automatic guarantee of salvation for some and an immutable destiny of damnation for others, there is much in the Bible which, if taken seriously, is a foil to all such theological outrages. For one thing, election in the Bible is constantly associated with the character of the God who does the electing, which in the New Testament is to be seen in the full revelation of the Father in the Son, who "is the image of the invisible God" and "bears the very stamp of his nature" (Col. 1:15; Heb. 1:3). The election of God, therefore, is not to be understood in the light of a syllogism based on a theoretical conception of the divine sovereignty, but rather is to be understood in the light of the revelation of the character of God in Jesus Christ. The first chapter of Ephesians is a happy hunting ground for predestinarian extremists, but it opens with a grand doxology: "Blessed be the God and Father of our Lord Jesus Christ" (1:3). The word "destined" is set in a context of loving Fatherhood, and whatever it means, it cannot mean anything which would do violence to the character of "the Father of our Lord Jesus Christ." The same phenomenon is to be seen in I Pet. 1:2, where the writer tells us that the struggling little Christian group were an "elect" people "according to the foreknowledge of God the Father" (K.J.V.). Again the election is controlled by the character of the Father God revealed in Jesus Christ the Son. The Scriptures are careful to balance God's action with his nature. God can never act out of accord with his nature revealed in Jesus Christ, or he would cease to be God. For that reason election must always be that of "the God and Father of our Lord Jesus Christ."

Again, election throughout the Bible is consistently related to service. Abraham was called not merely because he was a pet of the Almighty or because God had chosen to reveal His truth to him and to conceal it from the rest of mankind. In Gen. 12:2 the record of God's word to him says: "I will bless you . . . so that you will be a blessing. . . . And by you all the families of the earth will bless themselves." Abraham was called not merely to privilege, but to responsibility. He was blessed in order to be a blessing. He became the father of the chosen nation in order that ultimately all nations might be chosen. The same truth is made clear in relation to the Exodus experience under the leadership of Moses. God says: "I bore you on eagles' wings and brought you to myself" (19:4). Why? "You shall be to me a kingdom of priests" (19:6). They were chosen to be God's "own possession among all peoples" in order that they might be priests to all people, mediators to all men of the grace of God which they had known. A song current in the days of Micah and Isaiah gave more mature expression to this and serves to show the prophetic consciousness of Israel's election to mission.

The mountain of the house of the Lord shall be established as the highest of the mountains [in order that] all the nations shall flow to it, and many peoples shall come, and say: "Come, let us go up to the mountain of the Lord, to the house of the God of Jacob; that he may teach us his ways and that we may walk in his paths" (Isa. 2:2-3).

God's nation was to be the instrument of bringing salvation to all nations.

This is to be seen even more clearly in Deutero-Isaiah, where election and service are practically synonymous. Through Hebrew parallelism—"Israel, my servant, Jacob, whom I have chosen" (41:8)—choice and service are inseparably linked. And what was the service that Israel was to render? It was to witness by word and life to the one living and true God so that "the nations" should share in God's covenant with Israel. "I have given you as a covenant to the people, a light to the nations" (42:6). Through the covenant people all nations were to become people of the covenant. The New Testament bears this out when in the Epistle to the Ephesians the church is described as "destined . . . according to the purpose of his will, . . . according to his purpose which he set forth in Christ as a plan for the fullness of time, to unite all things in him, things in heaven and things on earth" (1:5, 9). Then the writer adds: "We who first hoped in Christ have been destined and appointed to live for the praise of his glory" (1:12). First Peter is even more explicit: "But you are a chosen race, a royal priesthood, a holy nation, God's own people, that you may declare the wonderful deeds of him who called you out of darkness into his marvellous light" (2:9).

When ancient Israel forgot the purpose of her election and thought of it in terms of privilege rather than responsibility, God had to break her as a potter breaks a vessel no longer useful. But this was because she had failed to fulfill the purpose for which she was called. The Fourth Gospel speaks the same word in regard to the Christian church. "You did not choose me," said Jesus, "but I chose you and appointed you" (15:16). Why? "That you should go and bear fruit" (15:16). The election is to service. But what if the service is not forthcoming? "Every branch of mine that bears no fruit, he takes away" (15:2). The biblical doctrine of election, then, is concerned not with an immutable decree of salvation or damnation, but with the call to God's people to share in God's purpose of redemption for the world. Election is finely balanced by that to which we are elected.

A further aspect of truth which is frequently related in scripture to the doctrine of election is the idea that the elect are called to holiness of life. I have known personally those who claimed that they were elected to eternal salvation by God's immutable decree, and because of this it was impossible for them to be lost, so that it made no difference what they did in the realm of behavior. And quite literally, it made no difference! Such a view comes from a lack of understanding the keen sense of balance which the Scriptures maintain at this point. To respond adequately to the call of God is to reflect the character of the God who has called us. Granted that the divine redemption is given us freely by God and is in no sense dependent on our works of merit, yet the evidence that one has accepted the unmerited favor of God is that gratitude prompts to obedience to his will and conformity to his character. "For I am the Lord who brought you up out of the land of Egypt, to be your God" (Lev. 11:45*a*). What then? "You shall therefore be holy, for I am holy" (Lev. 11:45*b*). To set one's self apart in exclusive dedication to God is the outcome of faith's grasp of redemption.

The New Testament is no less explicit at this point. Says Peter: "As he who called you is holy, be holy yourselves in all your conduct" (I Pet. 1:15). The conduct of the redeemed is to be a response worthy of the redemption. Paul more than confirms this when he writes in Rom. 8:29: "For those whom he foreknew he also predestined to be conformed to the image of his Son, in order that he might be the first-born among many brethren." Rather than predestination being of such a nature as to make moral behavior irrelevant, the very purpose of predestination is conformity to Christ! To be among the elect is to manifest the family characteristics of the family in which Jesus is the elder brother. Eph. 2:8-10 reminds us that we are saved by grace and that our good works are totally irrelevant in winning our salvation. Yet this significant word is added: "For we are his workmanship, created in Christ Jesus for good works, which God prepared beforehand, that we should walk in them." We do not work to gain God's favor; we work because we have God's favor. We do not work to be saved; rather we work because we are saved.

Although other examples of balance could well be discussed —such as the biblical conception of corporate personality as a corrective for an unbridled individuality, while at the same time stressing the exceeding worth of the individual in the group as a corrective for group behavior which is destructive to men's selfhood—enough has been said to indicate the delicate sense of balance which pervades the Holy Scriptures.

The second fundamental conviction, which grows naturally out of the first, is that biblical preaching ought to reflect the same wholesome quality of balance which is to be found in the scriptures on which it is based. The truth of biblical sermons should be biblically proportioned. The scriptures themselves should supply the restraints and set the limits within which truth, as presented in preaching, should move. In this way, man-made distortions of divine truth may be more nearly avoided, the weakness of overexaggeration overcome, and the wholeness of God's revelation released to make its full impact on men. At this point, as in others, biblical preaching is manifestly superior to preaching which is either vaguely related or wholly unrelated to the Scriptures, for the restricting and distorting tendencies of individual human minds may be transcended by the larger proportions and the complementary fullness of the entire biblical revelation.

A very practical question now arises out of our consideration of the balance of emphasis on truth. Since most passages of scripture contain a complex number of ideas, many of which are "harmonious opposites," is it necessary to bring into the sermon all these interrelated ideas? The obvious answer to this is: No. A sermon is not an exegesis; it is rather the fruit of exegesis. Consequently, more often than not, the actual sermon as preached will have to omit more than it includes of the fine points of exegetical research which enable the preacher to capture the delicate nuances which shape and control the particular emphasis on truth which should be presented. But in what is said in the preaching of the sermon, the same point of view should be maintained as would prevail if there were time to discuss all the details of the passage. The sermon, as it finally takes shape, should be the outgrowth of a grasp of the details of the whole passage in the mind of the preacher, so that what he finally produces for his congregation will reflect the careful balancing of one idea against another which has been done in the minister's workshop.

How much of the details of the larger relations out of which a truth emerges in Holy Scripture should be mentioned in a sermon will vary with the sermon and the preacher. There are times when the centralizing truth may be definitely related to its surrounding milieu by broad summaries, giving only the high lights of the larger context. At other times the sermon may be of such a nature that it will enhance the impression of the whole if a great many details are specifically pointed out which involve the intricate interrelations of thought in the passage. There may be other times when none of the details of the passage come in for consideration in the sermon. This allows for infinite variety of approach, and for the many variants of occasion, passage, or personal inclination of the preacher. But in any event, the truth which is presented to the congregation should reflect the delicate balance of the biblical materials on which it is based, which are clear to the mind of the preacher as he constructs the finished product.

One or two current examples of a failure to do this may help to clarify the principle involved. An advertisement published in a religious magazine some time ago carried across the top in bold-faced type these words: "THE SIN THAT

DAMNS." Underneath the caption was the following: "It is not murder. It is not robbery. It is not adultery. It is not embezzlement. It is not kidnapping. It is not drunkenness." All of this was then followed by the affirmation: "The sin that damns the human soul is—rejection of God's Son, the Lord Jesus Christ." The evidence for this was John 3:18—"He who believes in him is not condemned; but he who does not believe is condemned already."

This manifests lack of balance, exalting one phase of truth in the interests of emphasizing a pseudo-orthodoxy at the expense of other phases of truth equally valid. The implication of the advertisement to one who knows nothing of the Bible could well be that believing on Jesus Christ is all that matters, and that conduct therefore is irrelevant to Christian faith and experience. A pagan might well say: If murder and robbery and adultery do not damn, then it must be all right for Christians to murder, rob, and rape. But what do the Scriptures say elsewhere of these things? The devil, we are told, "was a murderer from the beginning" (John 8:44). "Any one who hates his brother is a murderer, and you know that no murderer has eternal life abiding in him" (I John 3:15). "But as . . . for murderers, . . . their lot shall be in the lake that burns with fire and brimstone, which is the second death" (Rev. 21:8). "Do not be deceived; neither the immoral, nor idolaters, nor adulterers, nor homosexuals, nor thieves, nor the greedy, nor drunkards, nor revilers, nor robbers will inherit the kingdom of God" (I Cor. 6:9-10). To balance the truth of the advertisement against the truths expressed in such passages as these gives quite a different picture. Murder, robbery, adultery, embezzlement, kidnapping, drunkenness, do damn, for unrepentant participants in such behavior do not inherit the kingdom of God.

Furthermore, the implications of the advertisement not only

violate such specific passages of scripture as those quoted, but they violate one of the fundamental truths of the whole biblical revelation—namely, that belief and life are inseparable. It may be replied that unbelief in Christ produces these evils, so that it is the unbelief which is really the heinous sin. It is equally true, however, that such evil deeds produce unbelief, and unbelief may well be the result of wrong behavior. The broader thought-relations of the very passage quoted in support of the fact that it is only unbelief which damns would have been a mighty corrective for this distortion, had they been consulted. For although the passage does say that one who does not believe is condemned "because he has not believed in the name of the only Son of God," it goes on to show that the root of the unbelief lay in evil deeds. "This is the judgment, that the light has come into the world, and men loved darkness rather than light"—why?—*"because their deeds were evil*. For every one who does evil hates the light, and does not come to the light, lest his deeds should be exposed" (John 3: 19-20). Here refusal to believe on the Son of God is traced directly to an unwillingness to have evil deeds exposed.

The inseparable relation between belief and deeds is further set forth in this passage when the writer speaks of him who believes as "he who does what is true" (3:21). Truth, therefore, is not merely something to be believed, but to be *done*. True belief and obedient behavior are here made practically synonymous. As R. H. Strachan says, this passage reveals "moral obliquity as the cause of unbelief." Frédéric Godet confirms this when he writes: "Unbelief is the night into which [the sinner] plunges in order to continue sinning. Such is the genesis of unbelief. . . . Faith . . . strikes its roots in the moral life." The "balance of harmonious opposites" in the passage itself is striking and if observed, would have afforded an ample corrective for the overemphasis indulged in for the purpose of exaggerating a particular brand of theological orthodoxy.

One further illustration may be to the point. A hypercritical mind recently appraised a Reformation Day address made by a leading American clergyman. Quotation was made of the following statement in the address: "But we go there upon the merits of Jesus Christ and our salvation rests, if you please, on our faith in that Christ who himself was sufficient for all." The editorial comment on this passage was interesting. "This statement," said the writer, "might appear to be absolutely all right, but there is one tragic flaw. Jesus Christ was sufficient for us all only in His *death*. Christ is not our Saviour by what He was; Christ is our Saviour by what He *did!* . . . We are not saved by faith in Christ—what He is; we are saved by faith in Christ—what He did."

But does what Christ *was* bear no relation to what he *did?* In a profound sense what he did was atoning only because of what he was. The whole meaning of the death of Christ centers in what he was. His death does not save us merely because he died. Everybody dies. Nor did his death save us because he died voluntarily when he might have escaped death. Countless martyrs have done that. Neither are we saved because he died on a cross. Thousands of Jews were crucified on crosses within a generation after Jesus' death, but they have no bearing on our salvation. Why is the death of Jesus unique? Because of what he was! It was the perfection of what he was which gave meaning to what he did. To set what he did over against what he was, then, is to betray an unbalanced understanding of the nature of Christ's work, one for which there is no biblical justification. When the writer of First Peter wants to tell us what Jesus did, he puts it in very vivid terms: "He himself bore our sins in his body on the tree" (2:24). But he prefaces these words with this: "He committed no sin; no guile was found on his lips. When he was reviled, he did not revile in return; when he suffered, he did not threaten; but he trusted to him who judges justly" (2:22-23). These words, expressive of what Jesus was, form the basis for the efficacy of what he did.

Illustrations could be multiplied indefinitely of the interpretive pitfall of faulty balance, but enough has been said to indicate that the Scriptures themselves, taken as a whole, and usually in their parts, are characterized by a delicacy of proportion and a blending of paradox through which truth is maintained in its wholeness. Biblical preaching should strive to reflect this, so that it may present "the whole counsel of God" and lead the hearers into the richness of a wholesome and proportioned faith.

V

BUILDING THE STRUCTURE

Development

Development involves the structure of the sermon. It is the point at which the things that are to be said about the theme must be built into an ordered whole. Development is to a sermon what architecture is to a building. It takes the materials of thought, as the architect utilizes the materials of his building, and arranges them in such a way as to give unity, coherence, and structural meaning. Development basically is the science of arrangement, the working out of the divisions and subdivisions of the sermon.

It may not be amiss at this point to suggest that sermons should have divisions of some sort. There is a cult of sermonic tricksters in our time whose aim seems to be to hide from the hearer the points at which an advance in thought is made. The reaction against the old "firstly," "secondly," and "thirdly"— or even "in the twenty-seventh place" of the ancient Puritans! —has led to a sort of streamlining of transitions and an automatic shifting of the homiletic gears which makes it impossible for the hearer to know at any particular time in just what gear the preacher is driving. In the early days of motoring, the shifting of the gears was a very clear-cut movement. The revolutions of the motor which had carried the car forward during its first stages slowed down. In the interval there was often a grinding of gears and a bit of a jerk as the clutch was released, and the motor took hold for the next stage of its progress. There was no question as to when each stage gave way to the next, and every passenger in the car knew exactly in what gear the car was functioning.

The automatic transmissions which have overcome this may be an automotive gain. It is questionable, however, whether there has been a parallel gain through silent-transmission homiletics. While riding in a car it may not be imperative that the rider know in what gear the mechanism is moving. But listening to a sermon ought not to be such a passive experience. Listening to a sermon involves conscious thought. It is impossible, therefore, for any automatic procedure of which the listener is not conscious to carry his thought forward from stage to stage and to get him from the starting point of the sermon to its goal. If the listener has to spend much of his time wondering whether the preacher has completed the stage of thought with which he began and has moved on to something else, or whether what he is saying at the moment is still relevant to the first stage of the sermon, confusion is bound to result and the final impact of the sermon be weakened.

This is especially true in spoken discourse. In reading, one may ask himself such a question and can leaf back a few pages, or even glance forward a few pages, to help him discover where the author has made his transitions and in what way the materials being read at the moment take their place in the structure of the whole. But in spoken discourse, where there is no opportunity for sustained reflective thought of this sort without at the same time interfering with the effort to follow the words of the speaker at the moment, clear signposts marking the stages of thought are a great aid to the hearer. And if some means is not used to mark transitions, the listener is likely to end with a confused understanding of the subject at hand.

Even in the most streamlined of modern buildings, where the ornamentation which once marked the stages between floors has been removed, the window lines still indicate clearly where each floor is. Or if the wall is solid, as is sometimes the case with air-conditioned buildings, the building can have no functional architectural meaning until the viewer steps inside and gets some grasp of where floor stands above floor and where stairs or elevator take him from one floor to another. A sermon without transitions, therefore, is likely to be a solid theological mass, perhaps quite as impressive as an unbroken twenty-story wall—and as meaningless. Phillips Brooks once remarked that the way to avoid the boniness of a skeleton is not to get rid of the skeleton, but to put flesh on it. The way, therefore, to give a sermon life is not to get rid of its points, but to make them as clear as possible and then to clothe the structural elements with flesh.

Granted, then, that a sermon should have development, that it should move from starting point to conclusion by appropriate stages of thought, what should determine the structural units on which it is built? What shall determine the points that are to be made in a sermon? Obviously, the basic starting point is that *the points should be an outgrowth of the passage of scripture on which they are based.* As was stated earlier, the theme of an expository sermon should reflect the theme of the passage which it seeks to set forth. The actual divisions of a sermon, therefore, should be divisions of *this theme,* and no other. To eat a pie, one must cut it into pieces and then bites. But it would be strange magic which could cut an apple pie into bites and transform them thereby into bites of cherry pie. So, when one divides a theme, each division should be a part of *that theme.*

The basic logic of this, however, is often honored more in the breach than in the keeping of it. One frequently hears sermons in which the development of thought bears no relation to the theme of the passage on which it allegedly rests. Ofttimes, even when the theme is adequately drawn from a passage, the things that are said in the development of the theme are quite unrelated to the things which the passage itself has to say about the theme. True exposition would necessarily build the structure of the sermon out of the biblical materials at hand. A sermon should embody God's truth. And the particular truth which it embodies should reflect the particular truth of the matter in hand.

For example, should one attempt a sermon on the whole Bible, obviously it would be quite impossible in one sermon to deal with every area of revealed truth. What then? The particular aspects of truth dealt with should reflect the grand centralizing or unifying elements of the entire biblical revelation. An organizing center, for instance, might well be the doctrine of the covenant, showing the development from the Old Covenant into the New Covenant and the permanent sense of unity between the two Covenants, as promise and fulfillment. One might well indicate, too, that although the New Covenant is the fulfillment of promise, it is at the same time a "promise of fulfillment." Just as the Old Covenant had elements in it which pointed beyond itself to the New Covenant, so the New Covenant has elements in it which are only partially fulfilled in the experience of the believer now. It holds out the promise of an increasing fulfillment in the ongoing of Christian experience throughout life and supremely in the life to come, when the pledge of our inheritance shall give way to its fullness. One could well indicate also, the central position of Jesus in the whole sweep of the biblical revelation. To him the Old Testament pointed forward. To him the New Testament witnesses in declaring his coming and in interpreting the meaning of his coming. On him our hope is centered not only as a past Redeemer but as the One who through all eternity shall abide as the Pioneer and Perfecter of our faith. Other centralizing features of the whole biblical revelation might well be selected around which to build the structure of a sermon on the entire Bible. But in any case, such a sermon should reflect the grand structural features of the Bible itself, and not deal merely with certain specific truths which are to be found here and there within its pages.

What is true for the entire Bible is likewise true for an individual book of the Bible or a chapter within a book or a paragraph within a chapter. The structural features should be true to the structural features of the materials on which the sermon is based. This does not mean, of course, that the final arrangement of the points in the sermon will slavishly follow the very order in which the ideas are introduced into the passage. There may be many times when for psychological reasons, or even for purposes of variety, there may be a rearrangement of truths by the preacher. One may impose, in that sense, his own structure on the passage. He may prefer to develop his sermon along psychological lines such as these: First, he may want to set the central truth with which he is dealing in the minds of his hearers. Then he may want to begin where his hearers are with regard to this truth at the present time. Then he may indicate where he wants his hearers to move—to show them the difference between where they are and where the full implications of the truth would land them. Then he will seek to motivate them, to make them want to pull up stakes where they are and move on to new and better territory.

This suggests that infinite variety is possible in the final structure of a sermon. The personality of the preacher, the needs of his people, the significance of the occasion, and a dozen other things will serve as stimulants to variety in sermon structure to avoid the monotony of sameness. But the basic conviction should underlie the preacher's whole effort that whatever the *form* of the sermon's final structure, its *content* will reflect the thought of the biblical materials on which it is based and will at every point be controlled by a careful analysis of the stages of thought as they lie in the passage under consideration. This means that before the preacher can adequately construct his sermon, he must carefully analyze the movement of thought in the materials on which his sermon is to be based, so that in the workshop of his own mind his own individuality will be controlled at every stage by the biblical thought. His outline may not be directly based on an analysis of the structure of his passage; it may rather be indirectly harmonious with it. But in any event it must be essentially harmonious. And should one fear monotony in sermon structure, he might well discover that an effort to make his outlines directly harmonious with the development of thought as it lies in the biblical passages themselves would go further toward correcting monotony than he could have imagined. For someone has remarked that the Bible is not marvelous for the number of its ideas, but for the infinite variety of ways in which it presents a few very great ideas. To reflect the Bible's own variety in successive sermons would, in most cases, be a more effective savior from monotony than the efforts of the preacher's own individuality.

Let us now turn to a passage of scripture to indicate how the development of thought in the passage should control the development of thought in the sermon. In I John 4:10 we see the marvel of God's love and its outreach toward men in mighty redemptive action. "In this is love, not that we loved God but that he loved us and sent his Son to be the expiation for our sins." Here we have set before us two tremendous truths of the Christian faith—God's love for men, and Christ's expiation for sin. It was God's love that sent Christ into the world, and it was Christ's redemptive work which manifested this love to men and made it redemptively effective. Now, in preparing a sermon on this passage, how shall the development of thought be arranged? In this, as in most instances, to answer this question rightly it will be necessary to search through the larger sweep of the apostle's thought of which this verse is a part, in order to capture the development of thought in the writer's mind. Verse 10 is embedded in the heart of a paragraph which begins: "Beloved, let us love one another." It is immediately followed by these words: "Beloved, if God so loved us, we also ought to love one another. . . . If we love one another . . . [God's] love is perfected in us." Furthermore, the next paragraph in the chapter includes the words: "We love, because he first loved us. If any one says, 'I love God,' and hates his brother, he is a liar; for he who does not love his brother whom he has seen, cannot love God whom he has not seen. And this commandment we have from him, that he who loves God should love his brother also" (I John 4:19-21).

An examination of these broader aspects of this passage immediately indicates that the major focus of the apostle's attention was on the supreme self-sacrifice with which we ought to love one another in the Christian fellowship. The costly love of God, therefore, manifested in the expiation of sin on the part of Christ, is brought into the passage as the source and pattern and stimulus of the Christian's love of his brother. Whatever the final form of the structure of a sermon on this passage, it would be true exposition *only* as it was controlled throughout by the end for which the words were originally written—that God's love for man becomes the measure and the ground of man's love to man. The ways by which this truth might be enforced on the hearts of the hearers could well be various. Different preachers would develop it differently, and the same preacher would possibly develop it differently on different occasions. But no matter by what stages of thought the final goal is reached, they must be pointing toward *this* goal and no other, and must necessarily be stages on the road that leads here.

Another example may help to make the point clear. Phil. 3:7 gives us the oft-quoted words: "But whatever gain I had, I counted as loss for the sake of Christ." Quite obviously the theme here is that the surpassing worth of Christ's love is such that all other cherished values pale into insignificance by comparison and are thereby to be surrendered to this higher claim. But how should the thought of the sermon be developed to enforce this theme? Should one abstract the text from the larger thought of which it is a part and develop it on his own, he might well find his mind turning in several suggestive directions. What are the cherished values that men hold dear which ought to be overcome by the power of Christ's love? Well, for one thing, earthly possessions. Did not Jesus say, "You cannot serve God and mammon"? Hence, the love of money must be surrendered to the love of Christ. Another cherished value of the natural man is pleasure, the indulgence of the flesh in countless forms. "The lust of the flesh and the lust of the eye and the pride of life" ought also to be consumed by the blazing heat of Christ's love. A third thing dear to men is social prominence. Another is power over one's fellow men, of one sort or another. Still another is love of ease and the avoidance of responsibility. These things which men call gain ought all to be re-evaluated and "counted as loss for the sake of Christ."

Now a sermon developed along these or kindred lines might well be a presentation of general Christian truth, but would not be an exposition of this text. And since there are texts which reinforce these other thoughts, why not choose them as the basis for preaching such truths? The text under consideration here is making no reference whatsoever to the natural man's common indulgences which compete for the love of Christ in his heart. I am inclined to think that Paul had given up most of them before he had ever known of Christ's love and that the surrender of such things was not much of a struggle for him. He was one of those rare souls who from his early years had his mind set on higher things than the ambitions of the ordinary man. His consuming passion for religion would have made the values of petty men seem despicable to him.

The things which Paul counted as "gain" were those things which he felt could be applied to his credit in his legalistic efforts to attain righteousness. He had many advantages, he felt, in his efforts to achieve status with God. If others could boast of background, training, or spiritual accomplishment as means of attaining right relations with God, he could outmatch them. He had the highest birth—a blue blood of the blue bloods among the Hebrews. He belonged to the religious party which could boast itself of the highest religious attainments—the Pharisees. His zeal for righteousness had been manifest in the fact that he had persecuted the Christian church, which he felt was blaspheming God. He had surpassed his fellows in his knowledge and his observance of the Jewish law, and could conscientiously and honestly claim that if righteousness were to be attained by legalistic effort, he was blameless. It was all this that Paul had counted as "gain," and it was *this* that he had come to count "as loss for the sake of Christ." He had surrendered all human achievement, had renounced whatever status was his by birth, had abandoned all claims to "a righteousness of [his] own, based on law." All self-effort and self-esteem had been forfeited that he might find "through faith in Christ, the righteousness from God." It was now his ambition not to present himself perfect in the sight of God, but to be presented perfect in Christ. Legalistic righteousness had been forever renounced, said he, in order "that I may know him and the power of his resurrection, and may share his sufferings, becoming like him in his death, that if possible I may attain the resurrection from the dead."

In order, therefore, rightly to understand and to develop Paul's thought here, it is necessary to feel the throb of the larger aspects of the passage which give meaning to verse 7. And although the final homiletic structure which a true expository sermon on this text might assume could well be as multiform as the ministers who preach on it, yet the content of the sermon would of necessity have to take into account the development of Paul's own thought and convey it to the hearers in its modern relevance, if the sermon were truly expository.

This recognition of the development of thought in a biblical passage is one of the most effective safeguards against the excesses of allowing the preacher's imagination free play. It does not stifle imagination, but bridles it so that its course is directed on the Bible's highway of thought rather than on the byways of the preacher's cleverness. Striking individual verses are kept in the perspective of large relations and thus saved from distortion. Psalm 121 may well serve as an example of this. What could not a clever preacher do with the suggestiveness of individual verses of this psalm? One can imagine a striking sermon on the subject, "The Slippery Foot," based on the words: "He will not let your foot be moved." Another might be developed on the subject, "Sun Stroke and Moon Sickness," from the words: "The sun shall not smite you by day, nor the moon by night." "From Exit to Entrance" might be another, suggested by the words: "Your going out and your coming in." Should any one of these capture the attention of a minister with a vivid imagination and the figure of speech be allowed to determine the development of the sermon, there could well follow striking results which might have no possible relationship to the centralizing and controlling element in the psalm itself. On the other hand, any one of these, if properly related to the development of thought within the psalm, might properly serve as the literary vehicle through which the real thought of the psalmist could be made relevant.

What is the central drive of the psalm? Its terminology is decisive in determining this. The expression "the Lord" or a synonym for it is used nine times in this short psalm. Furthermore, the word "keep" or its equivalent is used six times. On the other hand, the striking figures of speech concerning the "eyes," the "foot," "shade" from sun and moon, and so on, are each inserted but once. They, therefore, are inserted as a variety of ways of saying one thing. And that one thing is clearly stated in verse 5: "The Lord is your keeper." "God, our Keeper," then, is really the theme of the psalm, and the other elements of the psalm are poetic suggestions about the keeping power of the Almighty in the varied circumstances of life. They may all be drawn upon in the course of the sermon, but if kept in their proper relationship to the central theme of the psalm, they will be true to the intention of the psalmist and will also impart a sense of unity and wholeness by reinforcing the central drive of the entire psalm.

It may be well now to give a few examples of sermons which have been preached where the development of thought was out of accord with the passage on which they were allegedly based, to clarify the point by contrast. A sermon was once preached to young people on Eph. 4:1: "I . . . beg you to lead a life worthy of the calling to which you have been called." After stating that the theme was the worthy life, the minister immediately quoted an inscription on the Danforth Chapel at Berea College. This inscription, said he, reads something like this: "Dedicated to the worship of God with the prayer that here in communion with the highest the youth of Berea may acquire the spiritual power to aspire nobly, adventure daringly, serve humbly." He then proceeded to develop his sermon on the worthy life around this chapel inscription.

How does one live the worthy life?

I. Aspire nobly.

II. Adventure daringly.

III. Serve humbly.

These three phrases became the points of the sermon.

The difficulty with the sermon was that it purported to be a sermon on Eph. 4:1, whereas it turned out to be a sermon on the chapel inscription. The development of thought in Eph. 4 is quite different from that of the chapel inscription. And although it would be much more difficult to work out an outline on it which would be as clear and concise and appealing as the chapel inscription, it could be done, and the final content of the sermon would be much more distinctively Christian and much more deeply rooted in the gospel. Noble aspiration and daring adventure are not peculiarly Christian graces, and one might even find a good deal of humble service outside the range of the Christian faith. It is only as such characteristics are rooted in "the love of Christ which surpasses knowledge" and as those who strive after virtue attain "to mature manhood, to the measure of the stature of the fullness of Christ," that the truth of the Epistle to the Ephesians becomes incarnate.

Another example of missing the development of thought of a passage is to be seen in a sermon on II Sam. 16:11b: "Let him alone, and let him curse; for the Lord has bidden him." This verse climaxes a vivid story of brazen insult to King David. Absolom had led a revolt against his father, and David had to flee from his throne. Leaving Jerusalem, he went weeping and barefoot into the wilderness, in order to escape with his life. As he passed the summit of the Mount of Olives and came to the village of Bahurim, a man of the house of Saul, named Shimei, came running along a bank near where the royal procession was in retreat and began to curse David and throw stones at him. "Begone, begone, you man of blood, you worthless fellow!" he cried. "The Lord has avenged upon you all the blood of the house of Saul, in whose place you have reigned; and the Lord has given the kingdom into the hand of your son Absolom. See, your ruin is on you; for you are a man of blood." When he continued this verbal onslaught, Abishai said to David, "Why should this dead dog curse my lord the king? Let me go over and take off his head." The upshot of it all was that David, forbidding Abishai to attack Shimei, said among other things, the words of the text: "Let him alone, and let him curse; for the Lord has bidden him."

The theme which the preacher drew from this passage was "Taking Criticism in Your Stride." From one standpoint, this theme is a legitimate deduction from the passage, for certainly David was under severe criticism and he took it in his stride. We shall return to the question of the theme later. But for the moment, granting that the theme is valid, what was the development of thought through which it was reinforced and applied? The structure of the sermon was as follows:

One learns to take criticism in his stride in the following ways:

I. Learn that "you can't please everyone." (An old Latin proverb was quoted: "Not even Jupiter can please everybody," and the hearers were reminded that even Jesus had his critics. Therefore, we might as well steel ourselves to the fact of inevitable criticism and learn to take it in our stride.)

II. "We must avoid cultivating the martyr complex." There are those who are willing to accept criticism, nay, even welcome it, in order to satisfy a craving for sympathy from others.

III. Some practical suggestions as to how we may learn to take criticism in our stride.

    A. Learn to evaluate criticism for what it is worth. (There is true and there is false criticism. We must learn to distinguish between them.)

    B. Learn to profit by constructive criticism.

    C. Rise above destructive criticism.

    D. Seek, above all, to please God.

One of the striking features of the sermon was that there was no single mention of David following the introduction. If the development of thought in the preacher's mind was based on the passage with which he began, he took no means of indicating this in the preaching of the sermon. Furthermore, were the points made developed out of the biblical story about David and Shimei, or was this story a mere introduction to serve as a springboard for the preacher's own thought? Does the passage suggest that David said to himself: "Well, you can't please everybody, so I must forget about Shimei's curse"? Was David by his action seeking to illustrate the fact that he had no martyr complex? Had David learned properly to evaluate criticism and, above all, to strive to please God? There are some hints of these latter truths in the passage, for David said, "Let him curse; for the Lord has bidden him. . . . It may be that . . . the Lord will repay me with good for this cursing of me today." It would have strengthened the sermon if these points had been boldly sketched from the materials of the passage. But when all is said and done, does the thought of the passage really develop along the lines of learning to take criticism?

It was not criticism that David was facing; it was rather a political revolution in which both his throne and his life were at stake. And, said he, if "my own son seeks my life; how much more now may this Benjamite!" It was not surprising that an heir of Saul, to whose throne David had succeeded, should resent the loss of royal leadership from the house of Saul. And the question at stake now was not the bitter cursing of a disgruntled member of a rival dynasty, but the larger question of the right steps to take in quelling this treasonable uprising and saving the throne. There was a cause larger than David's personal hurts at the moment, and to that all attention had to be given. Furthermore, this collapse in the national life had stemmed from David's sin, and he was aware that it was a judgment of God. The outcome of events, therefore, was in the hands of God; and rather than stop to settle personal accounts with an insulting revolutionist, he would have to await God's action in developments and hope that the mercy of God would turn the course of events toward a final victory over insurrection.

The story of David and Shimei is not finished at this point either, and to interpret this scene adequately necessitates gathering up all the threads of the story and following them through to the end. In I Kings 2 there is recorded the account of David's death. As his life ebbed from him, he gave a final charge to his son Solomon, who was to reign in his stead. And the final recorded words of King David were these: "And there is also with you Shimei . . . who cursed me with a grievous curse on the day when I went to Mahanaim; . . . Now therefore hold him not guiltless, for you are a wise man; you will know what you ought to do to him." And just in case Solomon did not get the point, David added: "You shall bring his head down with blood to the grave." Taking criticism in his stride! Had David learned to do this? His dying breath was a charge to destroy the man who had cursed him! And before this chapter of First Kings ends, we find Solomon giving command to a soldier, who "went out and struck [Shimei] down, and he died." And the interpretation that the writer of the Kings puts on the whole incident is that the rivals of the house of David who had cursed him were themselves now under the curse of God, but "the throne of David shall be established before the Lord for ever." There is tremendous truth here concerning the divine election of the house of David, which leads forward to the messianic hope of an heir of David coming to deliver God's people. But it is doubtful whether the writer of the story ever intended us to draw thoughts from it concerning the taking of criticism in stride.

One more instance of missing the development of thought in a passage will suffice. There was once a sermon preached on Matt. 6:6: "But when you pray, go into your room and shut the door and pray to your Father who is in secret; and your Father who sees in secret will reward you." The points of the sermon were as follows:

I. Prayer is the secret spring of character.
II. Prayer is the secret source of power.
III. Prayer is the secret spring of peace and happiness.

Now, it is obvious on the surface that the only thing about these points which has any relation to the words of Jesus used as the text is the word "secret." For at this point in the Sermon on the Mount, Jesus was not discussing prayer as the spring of character, of power, and of peace. Rather, he was cautioning men about making a display of prayer, and utilizing acts of devotion for purposes of self-advertisement. It was this which characterized a degenerate Pharisaism at its worst, and Jesus

109

was seeking to cleanse the lives of his followers of such perversion. "Beware of practicing your piety before men in order to be seen by them," said Jesus, "for then you will have no reward from your Father who is in heaven." He illustrated what he meant from the three realms of piety of which many of the Pharisees made a public display—almsgiving, prayer, and fasting. Five times in the early verses of Matt. 6, Jesus used the expression "seen" or "praised by men." And the whole passage is based on a striking contrast. Acts of piety or devotion which are motivated by the desire to gain human approval cannot at the same time have the approval of God. The two are mutually exclusive, and the worshiper must decide which he prefers. He cannot have both. The passage, therefore, is not dealing with the fruits of prayer in human character, but rather with the motivation of prayer. Since true prayer is surrender to the will of God, one cannot engage in it in the same act which is designed to foster the will to human approval. The surrender of the ego and its exaltation cancel each other out. The development of a sermon from this text, to be true to the thought of the passage, would of necessity follow this general line of thought.

What we have been advocating in this discussion of development is that sermons should embody the basic conception which the very idea of development involves. *Webster's New International Dictionary* lists as one definition of development: "An expansion by means of which all the elements contained in a given concept are made explicit." In the case of a sermon, the "given concept" should be the theme of the portion of Scripture on which it is based. To develop this concept is to take the various elements of which it is composed, arrange them clearly and simply, and set them forth in such a way that the hearer has a grasp of this particular emphasis of scripture, and no other. The theme of a sermon should be the theme of the scripture on which it is based. This theme should be developed in harmony, either directly or indirectly, with the development of the passage in the biblical record. This would not seem to be asking too much from men whose task it is to be expositors of the Bible.

VI

CHOOSING THE TARGET

Purpose

———•◦•———

Benjamin R. Lacy once told of doing something in his early ministry which is always dangerous, but which ministers ought perhaps more often to have the courage to do—he ventured on Saturday night to read his Sunday morning sermon to his wife. When he had finished Mrs. Lacy said just one thing: "Ben, *why* are you going to preach that sermon?" Dr. Lacy confessed that the remark at first made him inwardly angry, for the companion of his life did not seem to be showing proper respect for his sermonic effort and was treating the product of his toil entirely too lightly! But without making any rebuttal, he went crestfallen back to his study. There he began to ask himself the question his wife had posed. "Just why am I going to preach this sermon?" he said to himself. And because he had not raised the question either before or during the process of preparation, he could find no reason which seemed adequate to justify his preaching the sermon. So, swallowing his pride and risking the possibility of coming to Sunday morning with nothing to preach, he threw his sermon into the wastebasket and burned midnight oil in hasty preparation of something entirely new which would enable him to give an intelligent answer to the question: Why are you going to preach that sermon?

Fortunate is the man who discovers thus early in his ministry that every sermon should have a specific purpose and that clear aim should be taken to achieve that goal. Otherwise he will fall into the habit of doing what the oft-quoted Archbishop Whately described as aiming at nothing, and hitting it! For it is tragically easy to hit nothing. And no matter how brilliant or clever or packed with content a sermon may be, if it does not have a clear purpose in view and if everything in it is not directed to the fulfillment of that purpose, it can be nothing but a "bewildered rhapsody," a "tragedy of aimlessness."

Preaching of this type reminds one of Beecher's hypothetical doctor who has been called to minister to a sick member of a family. He says to himself: "Well, I will leave something or other; I don't know; what shall I leave?" Then he "looks in his saddlebags to see what he has . . . got the most of, and prescribes it with no directions; the father, mother, and children may all take a little, and the servants may have the rest." The healing of spiritual disease will hardly result from such a purposeless handling of symptoms any more than would physical healing.

Bishop Boyd Carpenter once referred to "a dull uninteresting game" played in England called "Fishponds." He described it in this manner: "You attempt by means of something which is not a fishing-rod to pick up something which is not a fish." One could as well give the name "sermon" to a discourse which, by speech which is not directed to a specific end, attempts to achieve nothing in particular. It can at best be but a game and probably well deserves the epithet "dull and uninteresting." The advice of Alexander Pope is particularly essential for ministers:

> In every work regard the writer's end,
> Since none can compass more than they intend.

Let us now try to define what we mean by aim. How does

the *aim* of a sermon differ from the *theme* of a sermon? The difference is this: the theme involves the particular truth to be set forth in a sermon; the aim consists in what we desire that truth to do to the hearer, or what we desire the hearer to do in response to the truth. The theme is the subject; the aim is the object. There may be times when theme and aim are so closely related that it is difficult or impossible to distinguish between them. But there are many occasions when our preaching will be given a keener cutting edge if we keep clearly before our minds what we want the truth of our sermon to accomplish.

To state truth clearly is hardly a sufficient aim in preaching. That could make our sermons degenerate into mere intellectual exercises, whose aim is the logical arrangement of valid rational propositions and which may be evaluated like the correct answers in a copy book. Truth, however, is not an end in itself. Truth is an instrument by which living relations between God and the human soul are to be established.

One of the abiding insights which came from the Reformation is that truth is in order to goodness. To make the rational statement or apprehension of truth an end in itself is to make an idol of ideas in place of God. Biblical truth is not merely the correct phrasing of ideas. It involves that, but it is more than that. It involves the total response of the whole man to a personal God in such fashion that life that is eternal is born in the creatures of time, and the believer enters a new order of reality— the eternal order—and passes from the realm of corporate death in Adam to the realm of corporate life in Christ. When Jesus said, "I am the truth," he did not mean that he had come merely to add to the sum total of the world's stock of religious ideas and to formulate with finality all theological propositional truth. He meant rather that he had, from God's side, broken through the barriers which kept men from God, that he had restored the fullness of fellowship between God and man which sin had breached, that he had brought God's life to men. To preach Christian truth, then, is not merely to proclaim unflinchingly and without error the Christian doctrines. It is to aim at presenting those doctrines in such fashion that men may pass from darkness into light, from the realm of Satan's power into that of God's, and become members of the Kingdom of the Son of his love. And when the new life of the Kingdom begins to operate in men's lives, the aim of truth should be to nurture the new life until the soul in which Christ has been formed shall continually grow unto a measure of the stature of the fullness of Christ. Truth exists for these ends.

The purpose, therefore, differs from the theme as the surgeon's instrument differs from the outcome of his operation. He uses the instrument not merely to cut; he cuts in order to heal. The aim is to be distinguished from the theme as the lecture on heart disease differs from the cure of the heart patient. This difference between truth and the purpose of truth came home to me vividly in a personal experience many years ago. In the summer of 1935 I was traveling alone through the Near East. After sitting in the crude railway station near Ur of the Chaldees from the time I arrived at three o'clock in the morning until seven o'clock, I started out for the ruins more than a mile and a half away. I spurned the offers of a guide—since I had with me Sir Charles Woolley's book on the excavations which he had made— and set out alone across the hot, bleak sands toward the mound in which the ruins lay buried. I reached the ruins all right, but soon decided I had made a mistake in not taking a guide. It was entirely too hot to spend the whole of a July day there, and a hurried guided tour of the ruins would have given me sufficient background to spend the rest of the day reading Woolley's book in the shade of the station. I therefore started back to get a guide.

Almost immediately, however, the wind began to sweep across the desert with tremendous force, and soon the air was filled with sand. Suddenly it dawned upon me that I was wandering on a trackless desert in a sand storm in which I could not see three feet ahead of me. I was completely blinded, being unable to keep my eyes open in the swirling sand. I had to tie my handkerchief over my mouth and nose to strain the sand out of the air I breathed. Knowing how easily one can walk in circles and lose his sense of direction, and that I might as well wander off toward Persia as toward the railway station, the bleached bones of strayed animals that I had seen on the desert between Damascus and Baghdad became strangely vivid. I wondered whether future travelers would recognize that mine were human and not mere animal bones!

In my perplexity, a very simple but meaningful idea struck. Where was the sun? I opened my eyes momentarily and looked up. Soon I located the sun palely shining through the sand storm like a small disc of Swiss cheese. It was then about eight-thirty or nine o'clock in the morning. I knew that at that hour the sun was in the east. I knew also that the ruins lay to the right of the railway track from the direction I had arrived on the train. The train had been going south, so that meant that the ruins lay to the west of the tracks. My problem was then solved. The tracks lay to the east. At that hour the sun was in the east. Therefore, an occasional upward glance to keep the sun before me was all I needed to pilot me safely back to the railway, from whence I could locate the station. I heaved an inward sigh of relief, set off toward the sun, and within less than an hour was safely back at the station to await the next train at three o'clock the following morning.

For many years prior to that I had known that the sun was visible in the east in the early morning hours. That was truth, indisputable truth. But never before had it been living truth to me, nor had I ever made it purposeful. But in that hour the simple truth that the sun is to be seen in the east in the morning became more than mere truth. It became the instrument of saving my life! Just so, truth must become living and purposeful through our preaching before it can fulfill its intended role. We have insisted earlier that the themes of our sermons should be based on the truth revealed in Holy Scripture. But that in itself is not sufficient. We must face squarely the question: "To what purpose is this truth, and to what specific ends is it to be dedicated in this particular sermon?" The theme is the truth; the aim is that which we want the truth to accomplish.

There are certain values in having our aims clearly in mind in the preparation of our sermons. For one thing, it enables us to achieve a concentration of thought directed toward one end which will greatly enhance the possibility of making a decisive breakthrough at that point in the soul's defenses. Most parts of the bulwark behind which the soul hides from God are too solid to be broken through at one blow. All the resources of a week's study and of a lifetime of preparation behind this should, in any one sermon, be forged into one great instrument of attack; and this in turn should be directed in a series of successive strikes at one spot, and one only, in the citadel which we are seeking to storm for God.

The air hammers which are used to break up concrete roads are instructive here. Behind them lies a lot of machinery, designed to compress air until its force is invincible. But the whole of the air-compressing machinery is not used to crack the concrete. It rather creates sources of power which are all forced into one sharp tool in the hands of the operator. The irresistible force created by the compressor is all released at that one spot, the steel blade of the air hammer, not more than an inch long and a hair's breadth thick. And what is more, the mighty energies which propel that concentrated blade are kept pounding away at one specific spot until a breakthrough is made. An air hammer which is allowed to jump from here to there at random over a solid block of concrete will do little more than make surface pockmarks which deface, but do not accomplish anything.

This is instructive for preaching. All the compressed energies of God's truth which we have accumulated through the years should, on any particular Sunday morning, be forced through one sharp instrument designed to break through whatever area of soul-need that particular sermon is intended to fulfill. And what is more, the entire sermon must be a succession of blows at one particular spot until a breakthrough is made, rather than a desultory process of haphazard pock-marking on the citadel of the soul. Concentration of attack is vital to success.

John Watson (Ian Maclaren) once called this process of concentration "weaning an idea from its relatives." He said:

It is one thing for the preacher to woo and win a single idea, and to set up house with it in undisturbed company, and another to have all his wife's relations landed on him. . . . Take one sin that happens to be mine and other men's, and let the preacher confine himself, say, to pride, and it will be strange if he does not arrest and shame me, but let him throw in a dozen other sins and I shall be unmoved. . . . A sermon ought to be a monograph and not an encyclopedia, an agency for pushing one article, not a general store where one can purchase anything from a button to a coffin.

Limitation means concentration. If a sermon is to accomplish anything, it must accomplish *something*. It should, therefore, be like a microscope whose function it is to concentrate attention on a very narrow range of vision, but to enlarge and clarify this limited area so that many things about it which were heretofore invisible and unnoticed are brought to light and tinged with inescapable significance.

It is well, therefore, in spite of the fact that in preaching one is dealing usually with a broad cross section of humanity, to be very specific and to deal with individual needs. A master of one of the Yale colleges once remarked after a service in the Yale Chapel: "Preaching is like shooting quail. If you aim for all the birds, you hit none, but if you aim for one, you are likely to get several." It is quite likely, therefore, that in aiming at individual needs, we shall come nearer to meeting the needs of the whole group to whom we preach. This is true not only because the basic spiritual needs of men are quite the same, so that if we really lay bare the soul of one man his neighbor is likely to say, "That speaks to my need, too." It is true also because ofttimes the needs of individuals are best met in crowds.

There is a tendency in some quarters today to forget the value of individual therapy through group response. Some ministers are tending to give so much attention to personal counseling with individuals that the preaching of the gospel to a gathered congregation is belittled. One sometimes hears Dean Inge's famous stricture on preaching quoted with approval, when he likened it to spraying water over narrow-necked bottles. A few drops might now and again get through, but most of the bottles remain empty and dry. If people were bottles, the illustration would be apt. But people do not gather in church to sit side by side in mass isolation like inanimate bottles.

The conception is false from two standpoints. First, it is psychologically unsound. Listen to the wisdom of Phillips Brooks as to this:

A multitude of people gathered for a special purpose and absorbed for the time into a common interest has a new character which is not in any of the individuals which compose it. If you are a speaker addressing a crowd you feel that. You say things to them without hesitation that would seem either too bold or too simple to say to any man among them if you talked with him face to face. . . . You can see emotions run through the mass that no one man there would have deigned to show or submitted to feel if he could have helped it. . . . Imagine Peter the Hermit sitting down alone with a man to fire him up for a crusade.

Or, one might add, imagine the apostle Peter, when the crowd came together on the day of Pentecost, making an appointment with each one to see him individually in his study! There were no doubt many people with whom Peter thereafter counseled personally, but his Pentecost sermon did something for that assembled group that no amount of private interviewing could have accomplished.

It is often strangely possible for individuals to respond in a crowd in a way quite impossible when alone. Listen again to Phillips Brooks on this:

There is no doubt greater receptivity than there is in the individual. Many of the sources of antagonism are removed. The tendency to irritation is put to rest. The pride of argument is not there; . . . It is easier to give way when you sit undistinguished in an audience, and your next neighbor cannot see the moment when you yield. The surrender loses half its hardness when you have no sword to surrender and no flag to run down. And, besides all this, we have all felt how the silent multitude, in the midst of which we sit or stand, becomes ideal and heroic to us. We feel as if we were listening without prejudice, and responding unselfishly and nobly. So we are lifted up to our best by the buoyancy of the mass in which we have been merged.

Brooks's estimate of human nature here I take to be correct. It is psychologically true that individuals are often helped in a crowd more readily than they can be in personal dealings, and there are times when the power of the group can touch the individual with forces which can never be generated between two people alone in the counseling chamber.

But there is theological reason for this also. The New Testament doctrine of the church suggests that God's grace is given to individuals only by virtue of their incorporation into the corporate fellowship of the people of God. Individuals find healing through being ingrafted into the family of God, so that the health of the lifeblood of the group is imparted to them. Health of soul is to be found by losing one's life in Christ as a member of his body and by turning the focus of endeavor from one's own self-fulfillment to fulfilling the will and purpose of God through the fellowship and service of the church. Since this is so, it follows that God deigns to meet with his people in a special way in the gathered congregation of believers, and that there he fulfills the needs of individuals in a sense often impossible to them alone.

A French pastor, Pierre Marcel, has recently written: "Preaching communicates more than the most pertinent and convincing explanation given in private." He insists that this is so true that the preaching of the Word in a gathered congregation not only clarifies truth to the people, but even brings it home to the preacher in a way impossible for him to grasp in the privacy of his study. He writes:

A pastor prepares himself to preach and accomplishes the work that is his: reading, study from commentaries, reflection in communion with the church, prayer, anticipating the application needed for each one, etc. But he does not yet possess all that he will say, . . . *He is less rich than he is going to be.* In the presence of the faithful and with them, he too will have the experience of comprehending the meaning, the reach, the depth, the timeliness, and the vivacity of the message which he presents, better than during his preparation. . . . In the fellowship of the presence of the congregation he receives more than at his study table; often he suddenly understands what he had *never* grasped in the course of his studies, of his reflections and personal experiences.

One who has not experienced this has perhaps never really preached. God speaks to us often in the fellowship of his people a vitalizing word which is impossible under other circumstances. The specific needs of individuals, therefore, may often best be met by preaching to those specific needs, and herein lies a great value of clarity of aim and preciseness of purpose in the making of sermons.

Another value of this is its aid to the minister himself in the preparation of his sermons. Clarity of purpose enables him to concentrate his toil on a specific end and thus to avoid wasting a good deal of time in sermon preparation. To know precisely what one is going to do is to bend every effort right from the start to the doing of that one thing.

I once lived near a very gifted agricultural teacher. He knew all there was to be known about agriculture, but he would have starved to death on a farm. To know everything about a certain field of thought is almost as worthless as to know nothing, if one's broad knowledge is shrouded always in indefiniteness. I wanted to plant a lawn. So I consulted my friend several times about the requirements for producing a good lawn. Each time he bewildered me. There were, he told me, a dozen different possible combinations of seed. One combination did well in the spring, but not so well in the summer. Another would thrive if the season were rainy, another if the season were dry. Another was lovely to look at, but would not stand being walked upon so well. Still another would prosper in a certain type of soil and wither in another type of soil. Then, too, there were complications about cutting the grass. One type grew rapidly and tall and would need more frequent mowing, whereas another would require less constant care. Furthermore, one type required heavier seeding and more frequent reseeding. And as to the preparation of the soil, there were various combinations of fertilizer, each with its values and its limitations.

On two or three occasions my friend went over all this with me. But all he succeeded in doing was to paralyze my action. I had a plot of ground on which I hoped to build a lawn. Before I could get to work on it, I had to have specific ends toward which my efforts were to be directed. I had to discover what combination of fertilizer to buy to work into the soil, what combination of seed to purchase, and what quanities of each were needed. I finally, therefore, got my friend in a corner and pinned him down to give me specific percentages and amounts which I could write down on a paper. This done, I immediately directed action to these specific ends. The minister who succeeded me in that parish has been my enemy ever since, because the grass was so lush that he found it a burden to keep it cut!

Precise goals are likewise essential in the successful preparation of sermons. Until the wide range of one's knowledge can be channeled toward definite ends, the actual work of sermon preparation is paralyzed. R. W. Dale once remarked that "many young preachers, when they sit down to prepare a sermon, start like Abraham, who 'went out, not knowing whither he went.'" He added: "The preacher who has a definite end to reach, rarely loses any of the time which he gives to preparation; he sees in the distance the point to which he has to travel and he either finds or makes a road to it."

Dale reinforced his point by reminding us of the difficulty of pointless conversation with strangers. What should we talk about? Well, the weather is always the starting point, but we find that the one to whom we are talking has been as hot as we have been, and that subject is soon exhausted. Then we spar around to find out whether our conversationalist was at the concert last night, or whether, in the event of discovering that he had had a toothache, he goes to the same dentist we do and whether the drilling left him in the same state of collapse. And if we can discover that a member of the family broke a leg or had an operation, we eagerly seize upon that to consume ten minutes or so. And so the struggle goes on until we can make a break and get away. Said Dale:

But if we wish to secure some definite object, the difficulty of "making conversation" vanishes at once. . . . It is also true that while a preacher who simply wants to find something good and sensible to say to his congregation for half an hour . . . may be driven to his wits' ends to think of anything that is worth saying, a preacher who wants to get them to understand something which they do not understand clearly, or to do something, or to leave something undone, will find that the object he wants to gain will suggest what he ought to say, and the difficulty of preparing a sermon will be greatly lightened.

Since this is so, it is well to have one's aim in mind very early in the process of sermon preparation. It is necessary to know where one is going before he can plot the way to get there. When I am planning a long journey by car, I usually draw a straight line on a map from where I am to where I want to go. Then, I chart my journey over the roads which traverse the terrain nearest to that straight line. There are other considerations to be kept in mind, such as the smoothness of the roads, the hilliness of the terrain, or the beauty of the scenery en route. But other things being equal, the most direct line from origin to destination is the one to be chosen, especially when the purpose of the journey is to get there, rather than to saunter on a pleasure trip. The purpose of a sermon is not to entertain nor to amuse nor to astound. Its purpose is to set some spiritual goal and to get there. The best way to determine the path by which we are to go is to be clear right from the start as to our destination. We can then plot the journey with more ease and exactness and with more certainty of arriving. It is well, therefore, to heed the advice of Charles E. Jefferson when he said:

A clear cut aim is the preacher's life-preserver. . . . No question should be oftener on the preacher's lips than, "To what purpose is this?" That is the question with which he should begin every sermon. On the first page he should write in clean, terse Saxon the precise work which this particular sermon is intended to do; and on the last page he should write his honest answer to the question: Is this sermon so constructed as to be likely to accomplish the result for which it has been written?

The late James Black, the successor to Alexander Whyte at Free St. George's, Edinburgh, gave similar counsel to that of Dr. Jefferson, and followed it himself. He said: "If I may speak personally . . . the first thing I generally get is my 'conclusion,' *what I want to be at.* A wise traveller, in considering his journey, looks first to the goal. . . . In this case, the last should be first."

Two considerations reinforce the desirability of having one's goal in mind very early in the process of preparation. The first lies in the very nature of pulpit discourse. Archbishop Whately reminds us that in the pulpit we are not making an investigation to *discover* truth; we are rather *conveying* truth to others. In the process of seeking to discover truth, the end toward which we move will be uncertain at the start and will become clear only at the end of the process. But in the act of trying to convey truth to others, the conclusion must be present to the mind of him who makes the presentation right from the start.

The second consideration consists in the fact that if our final purpose is clearly in mind from the beginning, it will enable us to eliminate all extraneous material and to construct a sermon which at every stage is pointing directly toward the goal. There is a story of an artist who, upon hearing loud praise of some small object in the foreground of his picture, painted it out because it evidently detracted from the real message of the painting and was thus superfluous. To have a clear conception of the ultimate purpose of a sermon in the beginning of our preparation will enable us to eliminate all side issues, however interesting and valuable in themselves, which detract from the major message. Said Paul B. Bull: Aim should be "the test of all the means, the guide of every expansion, the judge of every illustration, the governing principle of every adornment."

In determining the purpose of an expository sermon, the controlling principle should be that *the purpose of the sermon should be the same as the purpose of the scripture on which it is based.* It is immaterial whether one begins with the scripture and draws the purpose of his sermon from it, or whether he chooses a purpose suggested not from scripture, but from a specific need in his congregation. If he is to be a true preacher of the Word of God, the preacher will, in the latter instance, search the Scriptures until he finds a passage the intention of which is commensurate with the aim which was originally suggested to him from nonbiblical sources. Wherever one begins, the final relevant question is whether what one proposes that his sermon shall accomplish is in harmony with some supreme intention set forth in Holy Scripture.

To answer this question will necessitate studying biblical passages in their broad relations, in order to determine as exactly as possible what purpose lay behind the writing of them. To use biblical passages for purposes not in harmony with those which prompted the writing of them is to misuse them. Stout once said:

The search for the reasons which led to the writing of the several parts of the Bible . . . is one of the first duties of the expositor. . . . For,—and it hardly seems to call for statement, much less for discussion—the reason for its being a part of the record is also the reason for preaching a sermon at all upon any passage.

Ofttimes, therefore, it is necessary to discover the purpose of an entire book in seeking to determine the purpose of a specific passage. Take, for example, the book of Job. There are many very marvelous passages in it to be found on the lips of Job's comforters. Should one fail to take into account the whole sweep of that marvelous poem, he might preach any number of inspiring sermons on choice phrases spoken by Job's friends. But should he do so, he would be running the danger of speaking a word of man and not a word of God. For in the end of the drama the Almighty says that all the thoughts expressed by Job's friends were false. "My wrath is kindled against you," said the Lord to Eliphaz, "and against your two friends; for you have not spoken of me what is right." Should we preach on the words of Job's comforters without allowing these words of the Almighty to control the purpose to which we put them, we should fall under the same condemnation.

Or take as another illustration the nineteenth psalm. The first verse of that psalm reads: "The heavens are telling the glory of God; and the firmament proclaims his handiwork." If one projected a sermon on these words, what should be his aim? If the text were isolated from its setting in the entire psalm, the purpose could well be to establish the fact of God's revelation in nature. Do you want to know God? If so, look into the heavens, read the hints in the glory of the stars, ponder the wonder and beauty and spaciousness of the firmament— and there you shall find God. This would be particularly appealing to the modern cult of nature worshipers who profess to find God not at church but on the golf course on Sunday morning.

But is that the purpose for which this verse was placed in

Ps. 19? The biblical writers never argued the existence of God, nor sought to prove it, nor did they seek to lead men to faith by seeing God in nature. About the best the Bible can do for those whose primary approach to God is through nature, is to grant that only God's power and his glory can be seen there, but not his redemption, and then to add that men refused even to believe in the glory and power of God revealed in nature and "exchanged the truth about God for a lie and worshiped and served the creature rather than the Creator" (Rom. 1:25). The writers of the Bible began with God's redemption at the Exodus, where faith in him as the living Lord of history and the Redeemer of his people was born. Then, after coming to faith in him as Redeemer, they moved on back to creation and concluded: "The God who redeemed us is the same God who created all things." Faith in the Bible moves from God revealed in redemption to God revealed in nature, never the other way. God's creative work is understood only through his redemptive word. Joseph Addison's famous hymn about "the spacious firmament on high" proclaiming the "great Original" by whom it was made may be legitimately sung only in a Christian setting. The faith makes a great deal of difference as to what one hears as sun, moon, and stars move "in solemn silence . . . 'round the dark terrestrial ball," as "no real voice nor sound amid their radiant orbs be found." They may "in reason's ear" rejoice and "utter forth a glorious voice" that "the hand that made us is divine," but "reason's ear" may just as easily hear nature saying something quite other than this. It is quite reasonable to the man redeemed by Christ to believe that nature publishes "the work of an almighty hand," but it may be quite as reasonable or more so to the man who does not know Christ's redemption, to see no God at all in nature, but to see the demonic, or nothing, behind it all.

What was the purpose for including the reference to God's

glory in nature in Ps. 19? The psalm as a whole gives the clue. Verses 1-6 indicate how the perfection of God is shown to the believer through the excellencies of nature. Then verses 7-10 show how the perfection of the divine character is to be seen in God's law. But the whole psalm moves toward the concluding verse: "Let the words of my mouth and the meditation of my heart be acceptable in thy sight, O Lord, my rock and my redeemer." It is the psalmist's concern that his life shall show forth the perfection of God which he sees in nature and in the law. Human life should glorify God as the believer feels that the inanimate world about him does and as does the revealed law of God to a devout soul. Hence, the psalmist prays to be delivered even from "hidden faults" of which he is not conscious, so that both his outward behavior and his inner intention shall be transcripts of the divine glory. The purpose, therefore, of a sermon on verse 1, concerning the heavens "telling the glory of God," should move toward the end of challenging human lives likewise to proclaim his handwork.

A good example of ignoring the purpose for which a passage of scripture was included in the Bible may be seen in the sermon of an old Puritan divine who preached on the Triumphal Entry. He bore down heavily on the ass who participated in the event and from it drew the following three points:

I. By nature every man is an ass.
II. As the ass was bridled and saddled, so grace bridles and saddles man.
III. The marvel of the Lord riding man in triumph.

The old preacher might almost have had biblical justification for his outline, for Point I is an admitted truism, Point II is a spiritualized interpretation of the passage, and Point III is an inference devoutly drawn! But what of his purpose? One look at the purpose behind the account of the Triumphal Entry would have spared the preacher his pains and the people his sermon.

Another illustration, not quite so ridiculous, but equally false to the purpose of the passages on which it was based, is to be seen in a sermon which combined two passages. We read in Matt. 10:29 that "two sparrows sold for a penny." Luke 12:6, however, indicates that "five sparrows sold for two pennies." The purpose of the sermon on these two passages brought together was to commend generosity, based on the example of the dealer who threw in the extra sparrow on the larger transaction! In this instance the preacher took aim at a target which never crossed the vision of the biblical writers of these passages, and one can be quite sure that he missed it!

One question must be faced, however, in this connection. Must the purpose of a sermon always be restricted to the major purpose of the portion of scripture on which it is based? Is it not possible that latent purposes in a passage of scripture are hidden behind the more obvious purpose? And are we not under the necessity often of enlarging or deepening a purpose or of applying scripture to ends which the biblical writers never faced? Paul, for example, knew nothing about the problems of democracy, he never heard of a labor union, and he knew nothing about modern automobiles and the terrible death rate they entail. Since, therefore, no passage of his ever purposed to bring divine truth to bear on these realms, are we unable to preach from Paul on the political responsibilities of citizens in a democratic state, or on capital and labor problems, or on the caution Christians should exercise behind the wheel of a car?

If this were so, then the limitations of our preaching would be intolerable. There are many areas of modern need with which the Bible writers did not deal directly, but to which their message must be adapted and applied. And the Holy Spirit, who quickened the writers of the ancient Word, desires to make it now a living vehicle of contemporary truth. But the Word and the Spirit must never be separated. The Holy Spirit speaks now through his Word, and not apart from it. Therefore, when we apply and adapt the Word to new situations, our purpose should never be out of harmony with the original purpose and most certainly should never be contrary to it. There is a difference, as James Coffin Stout has pointed out, between "deepening and widening," "applying and adapting," on the one hand, and *"changing* the purpose of a Scriptural passage" on the other.

At this point, as in many, I have gotten great help from P. T. Forsyth. He insisted that all great works of inspiration, whether in art or religion, transcend the "conscious horizon of the artist." We have the right, therefore, even the obligation, to broaden and deepen and apply the lessons of great creators in areas which go quite beyond the direct intention which motivated them. Forsyth seeks to safeguard the principle, however, by insisting that the interpreter is not free to use any meaning that he thinks he sees in a work, even if it should do violence to the original intention of the artist. He says:

We must indeed avoid and reprobate interpretations which are as alien to the original intention as the chief baker's three baskets are to the doctrine of the Trinity, or the "badgers' skins dyed red," in Exodus, are to the atonement. But while we refuse to do violence to the text, we must equally refuse to go no further than itself on its own road.

The words "on its own road" are the important ones here. To make from a passage of scripture an application of truth which leads us down an entirely different road from that traversed by the original writer is to do violence to the text. But to allow the biblical writer to set us on his road, then to pursue that road further in our time than was possible to him in his—this is entirely legitimate. So long as the broadening purpose is "really and reasonably congruous with its central idea," we may pursue truth to more distant ends than those reached by the original writers.

It was this which the New Testament writers did with the Old Testament. They saw that the roads traversed by the prophets did not end with the death of the prophets. These roads wound their way on down through the years until they ended in Jesus Christ. With profound insight, therefore, they reached back into the Old Testament to see Christian meanings which were not out of harmony in any sense with the prophetic meanings, but which saw more in them than the prophets themselves had seen. They carried further on its own road truth which was really and reasonably congruous with the central teaching of the prophets, who, had they lived to see the days of Jesus, would themselves have said: "This is what we meant!"

The justification for doing this they got from the risen Lord himself. In Luke 24 we see the risen Lord reaching back into the Old Testament not to find a few specific predictions which were mechanically fulfilled in the events of his life, death, and resurrection, but to lay hold on the whole Old Testament revelation as pointing toward him. "Beginning with Moses and all the prophets, he interpreted to them in all the scriptures the things concerning himself" (vs. 27). This Old Testament witness to him went clear beyond specific verses. The whole sweep of Old Testament thought had implicit meanings which he made explicit. Even the developing program of the church after him, he found foreshadowed in the Old Testament. "Then he opened their minds to understand the scriptures, and said to them, 'Thus it is written, that the Christ should suffer and on the third day rise from the dead, and that repentance and forgiveness of sins should be preached in his name to all nations, beginning from Jerusalem'" (vss. 45-47). Before the Resurrection the disciples would have been hard put to it to have found anything like this in the Old Testament. But the events of Jesus' life, death, and resurrection carried the Old Testament forward on its own road, and all that happened in the total Christ-event was "really and reasonably congruous" with the central intention of Old Testament religion. The New Covenant was not a different covenant; it was but a fulfillment of the Old Covenant. It was the releasing of purposes latent in the Old, which did no violence to prophetic thought.

This is not the place to pursue this subject at length. In recent days, however, many books and monographs have dealt with the relations between the two Testaments and with the specific problem of the use of the Old Testament by the New Testament writers. This is naturally an area of tension in biblical studies on which unanimity of judgment is not to be expected. It may be well here, however, to point out that it is becoming increasingly clear that the New Testament writers did not make haphazard use of the Old Testament, giving free rein to their individual idiosyncrasies in this regard, but were controlled by the judgment of the church which found in the Old Testament a series of profound correspondences between the redemptive action of God in the history of Israel and its climax in Jesus Christ.

The early Christians did not search the Old Testament, as some suppose, for mere verbal coincidences or fanciful "proof-texts" upon which they could call to justify their faith in Jesus. They believed that the God who had acted in him was the same God who acted in the Exodus recorded in the Old

Testament and in all the events which flowed from it in the history of Israel. They believed that this God had the end in view from the beginning. As a playwright works into the earlier scenes of his play certain ideas which are only perplexing at the time they are introduced, but which are made clear as one looks back to them from the standpoint of the climax, God was working into the earlier acts of the drama of redemption elements which, when recapitulated in a higher key in Jesus, received a clarity which they did not have in their original setting. Before we dismiss too quickly the New Testament writers' use of the Old Testament as fanciful or quaint or less worthy than our own understanding of it, we should at least try to probe beneath the surface of their thought, where we might find that they made a more profound use of the Old Testament than we had supposed. Exceptions to the rule may, no doubt, be found; but isolated instances do not discredit the central fact, and the marvel is that the exceptions are so infrequent.

To give but one example, the Gospel by Matthew is frequently cited as bristling with examples of a precritical and fanciful use of the Old Testament. Its author is sometimes accused of a rabbinic tendency to search the Old Testament for passages whose wording seemed to confirm his faith in Jesus, but the original meaning of which he quite bypassed. A favorite alleged instance of this is Matt. 2:15, where the flight of Jesus' parents into Egypt with their infant son, and their subsequent return, are interpreted as the fulfillment of "what the Lord had spoken by the prophet, 'Out of Egypt have I called my son.'" This is a quotation from Hos. 11:1, where obviously the prophet was making no predictions about Jesus, but was casting his eyes back over history to the Exodus, several centuries before his own time.

On the surface, it may look as though the writer of Matthew saw here nothing but a verbal correspondence upon which he seized as an Old Testament prediction of an event in the life of Jesus and thereby misused the passage. But is this a valid criticism of him? It would not seem to be asking too much to suppose that the New Testament writer was intelligent enough to see the problem he had created for his readers, if he were dealing with only surface meanings. Furthermore, even granted that the Jewish mind to which he may have been appealing was not averse to such use of Scripture, yet many of his readers were not believers in Jesus and could easily have discarded such an apologetic on the part of Matthew by the patent rebuttal that the Old Testament passage cited had nothing to do with Jesus. No, it is quite unlikely that the writer of the First Gospel was either so naïve in his use of the Old Testament or so lacking in astuteness as an apologist.

There is an element of profound theology wrapped up in the citation from Hosea here. Jesus himself had taught his followers that the scriptures of the Old Testament bore witness of him. And by citing the fact that his resurrection, an event of which no specific text speaks, was witnessed in the Old Testament, he indicated that the witness of the earlier scriptures did not lie in mere verbal statements. It was the Old Testament *as a whole,* in its record of all of God's redemptive activity in Israel, which bore witness to Jesus.

There is strong evidence to support the belief that Jesus found the pattern and meaning of his own life in the experience of Israel as recorded in the Old Testament. His corporate use of the term "Son of man," his use of the Old Testament scriptures in the crises of his life, his insistence that the Old Testament scriptures bore witness to him, and many other evidences besides, make this quite clear. It was Jesus' conviction that he embodied Israel in himself. What the old

135

Israel had failed to do, he, in their place, must do. He was "chosen" as they had been chosen. He was driven into the wilderness to wrestle out his destiny with God as they had been. He had a momentary success as they had had in the founding of their kingdom. He, as they, must suffer the loss of all, so that he could effect a mightier return from exile than they had known and finally through his resurrection establish a "kingdom that cannot be shaken." It seems unmistakable that both Jesus himself and the New Testament writers interpreted his career as the recapitulation and fulfillment of the destiny of Israel, and thought of the Christian church as the New Israel.

It was this theology which lay behind the First Gospel's citation of Hosea's word. Hosea was talking about God's unspeakable love of Israel when he drove them first of all into Egypt for their protection and nourishing, then later, after terrible suffering, gloriously delivered them from Egypt's bondage. In the flight of the baby Jesus into Egypt and his return, the New Testament writer sees the beginnings of a New Israel, which, but for the providence of God, would have been destroyed at its very inception. As the Old Israel, so the New, is set in a hostile environment. Her destiny is to suffer and be cast about among the nations. But the providence of God guides her through all her sufferings until, through her destruction, she rises once more to witness to the nations. Israel dies to live.

This citation of Hosea in Matthew, therefore, instead of being a mere fanciful use of Jewish exegesis, introduces right at the start the theology of the New Israel with regard to Jesus and the church. Here in this babe, the writer is saying, is the beginning of the fulfillment of Israel's destiny. All that Hosea was talking about in the Old Israel, both of judgment and of redemption, is now to be brought to completion in

136

this babe who is hardly alive before death casts its shadow over him. But follow through the whole Gospel to its end, where death gives way to resurrection. Then we hear the risen Lord saying to his church, "All authority in heaven and on earth has been given to me. Go therefore and make disciples of all nations. . . ." This is the final fulfillment of Israel's destiny. "All nations" are to flow to "the mountain of Jehovah's house" through the witness of the New Israel, until every knee bows and every tongue confesses that "Jesus Christ is Lord, to the glory of God the Father." In the First Gospel's use of Hosea, therefore, there is profounder thinking than that which discards it too readily.

Now it is the task of the modern preacher to take both Old and New Testaments and lay them down alongside modern life as God's word for this hour. In doing this, he will be frequently under the necessity of carrying further on its own road the thought of the Bible. Application will have to be made to immediate needs which are not specifically laid down in scripture. It is our task to aim at targets which may not be formally present in the Bible. But our aim must be taken from a biblical stance. Nowhere, for example, is slavery condemned outright in the Bible. It may be questioned whether Paul even dreamed of a society in which slavery was not a part of the social structure. But as P. T. Forsyth remarked, although Paul did not destroy slavery, his gospel did. Slavery was finally destroyed by releasing the revolutionary social dynamic implicit in Paul's Letter to Philemon and in the increasing application of the biblical insights that all men are created by God and are men for whom Jesus Christ has died.

But a word of caution must be given. It is necessary always, as has already been affirmed, to try to avoid missing or twisting the original intention of the biblical writers in our efforts to broaden, deepen, and apply. And it is quite possible, in our attempts to carry the original intention of a biblical writer further than he spoke in order to make his word relevant to our day, to miss the way by imposing a purpose of our own. This may be such a subtle thing that it is difficult to detect, even in our own thinking. That is why the deepening or expansion of the purpose of any biblical passage must be rigorously controlled by a wrestling with the *real* aim of the original writer—an aim which may have been deeper and more profound even than the specific end toward which it was directed at any one moment.

The glory of God and the coming of his Kingdom lie behind the specific goals of the biblical writers. Their momentary aim, therefore, must always be seen in the light of this larger purpose. In the days of Isaiah, for example, when Jerusalem was threatened by the Assyrians, the prophet boldly spoke forth the word of God: "Therefore thus says the Lord concerning the king of Assyria: He shall not come into this city, . . . for I will defend this city to save it." A century and more later when Jerusalem was again threatened, this time by the Chaldeans, the people recalled Isaiah's earlier message and applied it to their own crisis. "Is not Jerusalem God's city?" they asked: "And did not Isaiah say that because it is God's city and contains God's temple, it will not fall?" But Jeremiah had to shatter their false hopes based on Isaiah's words. "Do not trust," he cried, "in these deceptive words: 'This is the temple of the Lord, the temple of the Lord, the temple of the Lord.'" Jeremiah knew that the city was doomed, and the event vindicated him not long afterward.

Where the people of Jeremiah's day went wrong was in failing to see Isaiah's broader purpose behind the specific purpose of announcing the indestructibility of Jerusalem in his time. "I will defend this city to save it," Isaiah announced in the name of the Lord—but why? "For my own sake and for the sake of my servant David." The immediate purpose of the survival of the city was gathered up in the larger purpose of God's glory and the fulfillment of his covenant to David. The people of Jeremiah's time failed to penetrate to this more profound level in examining Isaiah's word. They transferred his specific word to their time, without understanding that for God's glory and the final fulfillment of his covenant it was now necessary that his city and temple be destroyed.

This suggests that in seeking to interpret the word of God to our day, we must be on our guard lest we draw false parallels without probing to the heart of a passage and discovering its deeper intent. In making applications to specific issues of our time which the biblical writers did not face, it is necessary to make sure that we do not unintentionally violate the original purpose of the scriptures which we are seeking to interpret.

An instance of where the carrying forward of biblical truth on its own road may be justified, but at the same time must be done with great caution, is in the application of the Scriptures to the problems of political democracy. The biblical writers knew nothing of the democratic forms of government under which we have been accustomed to live. And yet, it is quite commonly recognized that those who built the early structures of modern democracy received their inspiration and guidance from the Bible. It is easy to conclude, therefore, that the Bible stands for the democratic way of life, and to search its pages uncritically for materials to bolster a sagging democracy. Although the democratic form of government seems to be the form of human political arrangement in which the interests of the kingdom of God may best be served in our time, yet it must be kept in mind that the kingdom of God is more than the democratic State. It is to be remembered, too, that the Kingdom has survived many forms of political structure. It has had to manifest itself in various forms and at the same time sit in judgment on them. In our time the Kingdom is at work in the democracies, but it is likewise in judgment over them.

Furthermore, much of what we cherish in democratic life has no direct roots in the Bible. A freedom which is the inalienable right of man just because he is man is not championed in the Bible. Freedom, in the Bible, is a gift of God's grace to man and can be maintained only as it is the obverse side of accepting the absolute authority of God. As Forsyth reminded us years ago, the Kingdom is an "absolute monarchy," the rule of the crucified, risen, and ascended Lord, who demands obedience even to the point of bringing every thought into captivity to him before man can know any freedom. Democracy rests, too, on the will of the majority and often defines as right what the mass of men at any particular time affirms. The Scriptures never allow that right is to be determined by votes. Democracy often accepts the degree of civilization or culture of any society as the measure of the final good and often confuses inherited social customs and mores with the truth, whereas in the Bible civilization is usually the "world" which is the negation of the highest good. "The World, the mere mastery of nature and of man, is the chief obstacle to Christianity in the world," said Forsyth. And the great problem the church faces in this hour, as in every hour of world history, is to Christianize civilization, to subdue all human achievement to the kingdom of God, to fight again and again the battle first drawn in the Garden of Eden and dramatically recapitulated at the Tower of Babel, to keep man's knowledge and experience and power subject to the sovereign will of the Creator and used always as his gifts and for his ends. In preaching to a democratic society, the Bible must of necessity be carried further on its own road and be made to serve specific ends of which the original writers were not conscious. But in doing this, primary control must be exercised by the larger context of biblical truth, as well as the profound purposes which underlay the specific aims of the biblical writers, in order to be sure that our aims are congruous with theirs.

No set of rules may be formulated by which one may know easily and automatically whether—in enlarging, deepening, applying—he is true to the aim for which the scriptures exist. Sound exegesis of specific passages, a knowledge of the larger biblical context of which each passage is a part, historic perspective, and plain common sense, must be the guides here. But the Spirit who speaks through the Word will honor all efforts to allow the Bible to control the purposes to which it is put now.

Let us be purposeful in our preaching. Let us make our purposes consonant with those of Scripture. Let us when necessary go beyond the immediate intention of the biblical writers in applying or deepening truth, but let us never contradict or twist that original purpose. Let us allow the Scriptures to control our unbridled subjectivism in the enlarging and adapting and applying of truth to the ever-changing needs of modern life.

VII

RE-CREATING THE MOOD

Atmosphere

———•—•———

Atmosphere is necessary to life, whether it be physical life or the life of the mind. Thoughts, in order to live, must be set in an environment which permits them to breathe and gives them the quality of living organisms, rather than the stuffy, decorated death of museum pieces. A sermon is more than an arrangement of ideas. It involves a living encounter of living truth with living people. In order for it to live, it must embody an atmosphere which is vital and which in turn vitalizes.

Atmosphere is difficult to define. It is that elusive quality of either spoken or written discourse which gives tone and texture and catches up the listener or reader into a world created by the truth which becomes for the moment, at least, more real than the world of time and sense. It is an intangible quality—perhaps more tinged with imagination than with logic—which determines mood and reaches the deeps of the whole man. It is not mere emotion void of reason, for Wordsworth once said that "imagination is reason in its sublimest mood." It is reason, feeling, volition, in combination with an indefinable residue of reality which is vastly more than the sum total of each taken separately. Atmosphere in some sense is produced by the words used, but in a deeper sense arises out of that something which lies behind the words and goes deeper than they. It is a mystery which can be experienced, but which can hardly be put into words.

This subtle quality of reality is necessary to greatness in any realm of evoking human response. There are times in the realm of the arts when those who are technically perfect do not lay hold of men with the same force as others whose technique may leave flaws, but whose work is transcendently moving. Fritz Kreisler was perhaps not the best technician as a violinist, but, in spite of an occasional flaw, he could do with an audience what others with more perfect technique could not accomplish. His playing was characterized by that intangible quality which dug down into the corners of the soul and let light and air into areas of the inner life long buried beneath the debris of a sordid world. His secret is to be found in his own words:

I know a great deal about art, the technical side of it, as well as the interpretative, the mechanics and the artifices; but in the last analysis we must all fall back on the most primeval thrill, the thrill down the length of the spinal column. It is the primitive registering of impressions, and when I get such a thrill I know that what I am listening to or playing is all right. If I don't get it I know there is something wrong.

The vibration of what Alexandre Vinet called the "primitive chords of the soul" is the result of the power to create atmosphere. If it is present, a work is gripping. If it is lacking, it is dead. And technique alone cannot produce it.

One of the most marked instances of this I ever witnessed was in a concert given some years ago by the great violinist Yehudi Menuhin. There have been few violinists with his perfection of technique. On this occasion, throughout two thirds of a long concert, he played with flawless control of his instrument. The audience sat impressed with his skill, but unmoved by his music. They admired, but remained apathetic and dull. Near the beginning of the last group of numbers, however, something happened to Menuhin himself. He was using the same instrument and the same technique which had left his audience lifeless all evening, but from those strings began to come a touch of warmth and power which was like an invasion from another world. The deeps of his music began to call to the deeps of the hearts there listening. He lifted that audience out of themselves, until at the conclusion of that number, their applause was almost hysterical. It was a moment I shall never forget as long as I live.

What made the difference? It was the same audience, the same player, the same violin, the same general sort of music. But something happened to the player himself. Insofar as an observer can read the behavior of another, it appeared that Menuhin, who earlier in the evening appeared detached and impersonal, became interested in his music and his audience and began to respond himself to the mood of the music he was playing. He yielded himself to the spell of what the composer had created and thus became the medium of re-creating the mood of the music for the listeners. His own soul was quickened into life by the music and began to pour itself out through his instrument. He was transformed from a technically perfect performer into a living creator of music which had in it the subtle touch of heaven. The transformed mood of the player caught up the whole audience and went racing through their hearts like fire. One cannot quite define the difference, but to have experienced it was a privilege seldom granted to a man.

What is true of music is true also of speech. The power to move men goes beyond the mere words one uses, beyond all techniques which can be consciously acquired, beyond all striving for effect. And masters in the art of speech know the difference between success and failure at this point. George Arliss described the difference as that between "interesting" and "thrilling." One of the plays in which he acted, *Paganini,* he described as "a most charming production—picturesque and attractive in both costume and scenery." But when his friends gathered round him after the first performance, he confessed: "We all knew there was something wrong. I felt it when the curtain fell. And when my friends beamed at me and said 'Most interesting!' I knew I hadn't struck a success." He continued, "Interesting! Fatal word. Nobody ever told me *The Green Goddess* was interesting. 'How thrilling!' was the expression used there. That meant success. But 'Interesting!' So, I've no doubt, is an operation for appendicitis."

If it is true in the realm of the arts, it is supremely true in preaching, that truth must come alive, lifting the hearer out of himself and gripping him with a force which he cannot easily shake. It is the task of the preacher to try to create a mood which shall carry the listener beyond the mere words he speaks to the transcendent realities with which the gospel deals. It may not be given to many of us to have the native gifts of eloquence which could enable George Whitefield to make men rise to their feet to man lifeboats as he described the sinking of a ship, or which caused men to cast involuntary looks back over their shoulders as Alexander Whyte described the hounds of hell pursuing them because of their sin. But after we have done our best to capture the meaning of a passage of scripture, we should then seek to convey its mood in such a way that the hearer becomes a participant in the issues with which the Bible deals. Someone said of John Cotton, "When he preaches out of any prophet or apostle, I hear not him, but that very prophet and apostle; yea, I hear the Lord Jesus

Christ himself speaking in my heart." It is that for which we must strive.

How is this to be done? Two suggestions may be appropriate here. First, it may be well to cultivate the imagination until one is enabled to enter into the biblical scenes and feel the throb of the heartbeat of the biblical characters. We must seek not only to discover the truth, but also to relive the truth until it becomes a part of us. This was one of the secrets of the effectiveness of Alexander Whyte's preaching. He held that knowledge and ideas formed the content of the message, but before the message could become power it "must be fused by the glow of personal experience and lit up by the flash of imagination." On long, solitary walks during his holidays and in the quiet of his study hours, he spent a great deal of time brooding over the themes and characters on which he planned to preach and tried to live with them until they became as real to him as were his neighbors or his family. He regarded the imagination as "nothing less than the noblest intellectual attribute of the human mind" and deliberately cultivated all the native gifts of imagination that he had. It would be well for any preacher to stimulate the imagination and to increase it by exercise.

The second suggestion is that this should be rooted in prolonged and intimate touch with the passage of scripture on which one is planning to preach. Hawthorne's principle in "The Great Stone Face," that one in some measure becomes like that on which he gazes at length, is eminently true here. Most scripture passages have a distinct mood or tone. If one lives on friendly enough terms with his passage, he is likely to capture—or better, be captured by—its atmosphere and reflect something of it in the pulpit. This cannot be done by hurried and frenzied last-minute efforts to get "something to say." It can usually come only when the pressure is off, the mind is free of fretfulness, and there is time to absorb, listen, meditate.

Meditation is almost a lost art with us. The demands on our time are appalling. It is difficult to avoid interruptions. The call of the sick and the wayward is so urgent that if we sit down for a time just to think or brood, we almost have a feeling of guilt. But if we get our sermons on the run, they will hardly smack of the mood of eternity. Harris E. Kirk once told of sitting alone with his grandson by the fireside in his library one winter's night. Kirk was brooding, and finally the grandson broke the silence: "Grandfather, what are you doing?"

"I am thinking, my boy," came the reply.

But this seemed to make no sense to the grandson, who pressed his question again: "But Grandfather, what are you doing?"

To which Kirk replied, "My boy, sometimes just thinking is doing." He commented later that he wondered what would become of a generation who did not know that sometimes just thinking is doing. That is a lesson which we need to relearn in our time.

When we set about to deal seriously with atmosphere in our preaching, the simple principle should be in control that our sermons should reflect the atmosphere of the passages on which they are based. By prolonged study and absorption, the tone of the scripture we are studying will almost automatically impart itself to us, so that when we deal with the passage in the pulpit we shall convey the mood which the scripture has kindled in us. But to do this, our study must include not only ideas—it must be a search for the subtle quality of reality which gives life to the passage. Some passages reflect a mood of judgment, some of courage, some of quiet confidence, others of righteous indignation at some wrong. A truly expository sermon should reflect, and re-create in the hearers, whatever is the mood of the passage.

As Marvin R. Vincent has put it:

The expositor must . . . aim to put himself for the time into the very *atmosphere* and *spirit* of the age out of which the Word comes; not only to know, but to *feel* the motives of its acts and sayings. He must catch the quality of Jacob's shrewdness; he must glow with Deborah's warlike ardor; he must appreciate the political sagacity, no less than the fatherly tenderness of Jephthah; he must thrill, like the singers of the Pilgrim Psalms, with inspiring and mournful memories of Jerusalem; he must be touched with the grateful affection which overflows in Paul's letter to the Philippians, and burn with the righteous indignation of his words to the Galatians and Corinthians.

As the preacher puts himself into these various situations, he will tend to carry his hearers with him.

It is very easy to miss the atmosphere of a passage and to substitute another of our own if care is not taken to avoid this. For example, a sermon was once preached on a part of Rom. 5:8, dealing with the subject of sin: "While we were yet sinners Christ died for us." The burden of the sermon was unsparing condemnation of our sin—sin black and heinous enough to cause the death of Christ. The mood of this great passage, however, is quite other than this. The early part of the very passage from which the text was taken tells us that "God shows his love for us in that while we were yet sinners Christ died for us." Furthermore, the chapter opens on a note of glorious justification whereby we have "peace with God," and the paragraph from which the text comes closes, "We also rejoice in God through our Lord Jesus Christ, through whom we have now received our reconciliation." The word "rejoice" is one of the key words, if not the key word, in the whole passage, and the accompanying words are "peace," "grace," "hope," "love," "saved," "reconciled." Although Paul did at times engage in unsparing condemnation of sin, in this passage his mood is one of exultation and joy over the fact that God's love is greater than man's sin, and that through the death of Christ a reconciliation has been effected which is more than a match for the deepest blackness of human perversion. A sermon on sin from this passage, therefore, should re-create this mood of rejoicing over the fact that it has been conquered by God's love.

Another instance of faulty atmosphere is to be seen in a sermon on Acts 2:42: "And they devoted themselves to the apostles' teaching and fellowship, to the breaking of bread and the prayers." The outline came right out of the passage, each point reflecting one facet of the life of the apostolic church set forth here. The points were:

I. Teaching.

II. Fellowship.

III. Breaking of bread.

IV. Prayer.

In the developing of these points, however, the preacher in each case intruded an element of rebuke. In discussing teaching, stress was laid on the failure of the modern church to know and teach its faith. The remarks on fellowship were directed toward our withholding of what we ought to give one another as members of the body of Christ. The same tone of judgment prevailed throughout the sermon.

The marked lack here was the failure to reproduce the atmosphere of the scripture on which the sermon was based. The passage in Acts has a certain exuberance of spirit; it gives one a sense of uplift and triumph. The sermon, on the other hand, was a rebuke for failure to do our duty. The passage is a call from above to come up higher. The sermon was rather a push from below to go up higher. In discussing teaching in this context, it would have been more suitable to dwell on the surpassing excellence of the teaching which had brought this group into being and had sent them forth into the world with the breathtaking "good news" of the Resurrection. In dealing with fellowship, a setting forth of the life enrichment of the common faith which these people had found would have been more appropriate in this setting. The mood should have been one not of judgment, but rather of wonder and amazement at the tremendousness of the "good news" by which these people had been captured and at the sudden growth which added to their numbers. The minister had taken his stance more within the lethargy and drabness of the modern church than within the freshness and exuberance of the apostolic church.

It is well always to examine the terminology of the larger reaches of a passage, to brood over it until its tone pervades our own thinking and feeling, to let the imagination roam through the setting of the ancient story and through the feelings of the biblical characters, until the atmosphere in which the original story was enacted or written lays hold of us and is reflected in our treatment of it. Thomas a Kempis once wrote: "Each part of Scripture is to be read in the same spirit in which it was written." This might be paraphrased to read: "Each part of scripture should be preached in the same atmosphere in which it was written."

A problem arises in this connection. Do not certain passages of scripture reflect changing moods? If so, how shall this be reflected in preaching? It is true that some passages combine various moods and change as they move along. And sometimes it is difficult to tell just what sort of mood one should try to reflect in preaching on such passages. It is usually the case, however, that the changing facets are in the details of the passage, with a major mood pervading the whole. Sometimes the changes are introduced as foils to the main tone of the story, in order, by contrast, to enhance the effect of the tone of the whole. In this case, the ideal sermon would likewise move through changing moods, so that each facet of the atmosphere of the passage could be called on to enhance the impact of the central drive. If such an ideal is beyond us, then it would perhaps be best, in any case, to search for the controlling tone and allow it to set the tone of the sermon.

This difficulty is faced when one attempts a sermon on such a passage as John 3:16. Here it is the marvelous love of God which is the central drive of the passage, and the major mood is one of wooing and gentle entreaty. The passage moves on, however, to speak of judgment. "He who does not believe is condemned . . . and this is the judgment, that the light has come into the world, and men loved darkness rather than light, because their deeds were evil." In making an appeal for decision, the passage confronts the reader both with the high possibilities of redemption and the fearful consequences of judgment for those who deliberately reject that redemption. How should one's sermon on this passage end? By holding up the wonder of the deliverance, or the fearfulness of turning one's back on it? It is likely that one may decide this question on psychological grounds, trying to determine which is most calculated to motivate the hearer to action. It is quite possible that the same preacher might change tactics here on the same sermon to different audiences. The spiritual condition of a congregation, the tone of the whole service, the gentle pressures of the Spirit's presence, could well be decisive in making one or the other of these approaches appropriate on any given occasion.

But whichever ground of appeal is finally taken, there is little doubt that the larger tone of this third chapter of John is that of the wonder of God's love and the marvel of redemption. If, therefore, one should choose to end with a note of warning, still this should be done in the light of how rejection of the light is a denial of God's love and a fearful betrayal of the Redeemer who has wrought salvation at such infinite cost. So the same general mood would prevail, whichever tactic was adopted to clinch the sermon.

A definite part of our task as preachers is to re-create moods from scripture, to make our congregation feel the force of the truth which we present. This is no easy task. Sometimes it is an impossible one. Amelita Galli-Curci is reported to have said: "There is no such thing as a 'cold' audience. Your audience is what you make it." She was a singer, not a preacher. She had audiences, not congregations. Had she ever had to try to break through the icy indifference of some gatherings for worship, she would have used more guarded words. Even Alexander Whyte once confessed to having been frozen so thoroughly by a congregation that he did not thaw out for months afterward! A singer usually has the co-operation of the natural man. The natural man is the preacher's obstacle. The world and the flesh, if not the devil, are on the side of the entertainer, whereas they are all arrayed against the preacher. But granting all that, still it is true, within limits at least, that a congregation "is what you make it." Galli-Curci added: "But you must touch the heart! And to reach the heart of an audience your own mood must not be cold. . . . Being a singer is not a career with me. It is a necessity. Ever since babyhood I have sung, simply because my voice would bubble forth." Perhaps that is the secret. When preaching is no longer a career, but a necessity; when we are so gripped by the truth of the gospel that there is a spontaneous bubbling forth of life and power as we preach; then more of our cold congregations will be quickened, and the glow of heaven light the darkness of earth's way.

Fire is kindled by fire. Let us capture the Bible's fire and lay it on the dry fagots of our own lives and those of our own people. The world needs to know again that "our God is a consuming fire."

INDEX
OF SCRIPTURE REFERENCES

INDEX OF SCRIPTURE REFERENCES

INDEX
OF PERSONS AND SUBJECTS

156